*A Literi
of Old Lonaon*

THE ROYAL & BISHOPS' PALACES IN OLD LONDON

WITH THE PARLIAMENT HOUSES
AND COURTS OF JUSTICE AND
THE GREAT HOUSES OF THE
NOBLES & STATESMEN

FOUNDED MAINLY ON ALLUSIONS IN
SIXTEENTH AND SEVENTEENTH CENTURY
LITERATURE

BY

WILBERFORCE JENKINSON

AUTHOR OF 'LONDON CHURCHES BEFORE
THE GREAT FIRE'

LONDON
SOCIETY FOR PROMOTING CHRISTIAN KNOWLEDGE
NEW YORK: THE MACMILLAN COMPANY
1921

BY THE SAME AUTHOR

LONDON CHURCHES
BEFORE THE GREAT FIRE

FOUNDED mainly on allusions in 16th and 17th century literature, to which are added some historical notes, with twenty reproductions, in collotype, of old prints and drawings in the British Museum, by Mr EMERY WALKER. 15s net.

The Contemporary Review says: 'Mr Jenkinson has done excellent work in producing this noble volume.'

The English Historical Review says: 'An especially delightful feature is its large number of admirable reproductions of old engravings, for the most part of churches now destroyed.'

The Daily Telegraph says: 'Mr Wilberforce Jenkinson deserves the gratitude of all lovers of London'

LONDON : S P.C.K.

Preface

IN offering my prospective readers a further work on Old London before the Great Fire, I am following the lines adopted in my former book on the Churches published some three years ago, viz., to illustrate the subjects treated as much as possible by quotations, taken mainly from 16th and 17th century literature, though not neglecting the best known authors of an earlier period and the old Chroniclers. I have, moreover, used freely the Calendars of State Papers and Patent Rolls, and other like Records printed in the Rolls Series. As before, I have made extensive use of the Poets and Dramatists: with regard to the latter the citations used would be more numerous were the scenes of the plays laid in London, but in the majority of cases this is not so, with the exception, perhaps, of Ben Jonson, a London-bred man, who found as much of the romantic element in the scenes and life of his native place as is to be imagined in France, Italy, or Spain. I have used, wherever available, the scarce early plays and tracts not well known, and which are to be found for the most part in the British Museum or in Sion College Library, or, in the case of plays, in the Malone Collection at the Bodleian Library or the Dyce Collection at South Kensington. The Garrick Plays are at the British Museum. Letters and Biographies have proved of great service, and have been used where accessible. I have quoted freely from John Stow's great work, 'A Survey of London,' first published in 1598, and have used the text of the best edition, that of 1603, as reprinted and edited by Mr. E. C. L. Kingsford, and in my references I have given the page numbers of the 1603 edition as supplied by the Editor. Students of Stow are much indebted to Mr.

A LITERARY TOPOGRAPHY OF OLD LONDON

Kingsford for so complete and learnedly annotated an edition of the great topographer.

Thanks are due to the Editor for kind permission to reprint the article on the Bishops' Houses, which appeared in the *Church Quarterly Review*; also to the Rev. Claude Jenkins, Librarian at Lambeth Palace and Professor of Ecclesiastical History at King's College, London, for friendly suggestions, especially with regard to the section on Lambeth Palace.

My work is not a History nor a Dictionary it aims no higher than to provide an anthology of references in early literature to old London palaces and, incidentally, to men who lived there To take one instance only, I give the reader what references I can find to the Parliament Houses, but the real history of the High Court of Parliament as a British Institution, which has been treated by abler pens than mine,[1] and some incidents connected therewith, I barely touch I trust, however, that the book may prove a useful appendix to the more elaborate work of the historian.

I have not studied scrupulously to follow in all cases an orderly sequence, either topographical or chronological, and the precise reader may find a cause for censure and accuse me of a wandering habit To this I plead guilty, and can only apologise in the words of an old traveller:

'If my thoughts have wandred I must intreat the wel-bred Reader to remember I have wandred through many deserts.'[2]

WILBERFORCE JENKINSON.

[1] Notably by Professor A F Pollard in his recent work, not published till after this book was in the press
[2] Sir Thomas Herbert, *Travels*, 1634.

Prelude

IN PRAISE OF LONDON

LONDON, the 'Troynovant' of legendary history, has no lack of poets to sing its praise.

> New Troy my name when first my fame begun
> By Trojan Brute who first me placed here,
> On fruitful soyle where pleasant Thames doth run

These lines are inscribed on the well-known early map of London by Agas, but the writer continues:

> Sith Lud my Lord, my King and Lover dear
> Encreased my bounds and London
> ... he called then my name,

and thus supports the theory of a fabulous King Lud. Robert Chester has almost the same words:

> Lud the great King did with his wealth enlarge
> The famous builded Citie.[1]

Camden, whom we are bound to take seriously, speaks with caution:

> I am almost of opinion that London was by way of eminence simply call'd *the City*, or *the City in a wood*,

but he asks leave to 'guess once more,' and he suggests a

name from that which was the original both of its growth and glory; I mean Ships, call'd by the British *Lhong*; so that London is as much as a *Harbour* or *City of Ships*.[2]

---

[1] *Love's Martyr*, 1601. This is the derivation given in the early chronicle known as *Brut* (c 1400): 'Called the Citee of Ludstan: but now that name is chaunged throu3 variance of letters and now is called London.'

[2] 1586. *Britannia* (1722), i. 370.

A LITERARY TOPOGRAPHY OF OLD LONDON

Sir William Davenant has a somewhat fanciful definition:

> As the name
> Of London from the great Diana came,
> So, that it was with this word Lin, put to,
> Which signifies a Pool, where waters doe
> As here they did, cause lakes: and this is plain,
> Because the Tames near part doth still retain,
> The title of the Pool, Llyn-Tain is then
> A town there fixt, where to Diana, men
> Had hallowed a 'lake'...
> 'Lhan' a temple is and 'Tain' Diana [1]

Tacitus uses the Roman name Londinium, and Nennius 700 years later 'Cair Londein.' In the 'Mabinogion' (c. 1300) Lwndrys is the word used.[2]

It is impossible to give all the varied and fanciful derivations of the name of London. An early poet uses the word Troy, only in a metaphorical sense

> London thou art of Townes *A per se*
> Strong Troy in vigour and in strenytie.[3]

For the London-born man the City always had something of enchantment.

> The sight of London to my exiled eyes
> Is as Elysium to a new come soul.

So speaks a Londoner in Marlowe's 'Edward II.'[4] Herrick calls it his 'Native Countrey.'[5] Euphues, with something of rapture, describes it as:

> A place both for the beauties of buylding, infinite riches, varietie of all things, that excelleth all the Cities in the World; insomuch that it may be called the Storehouse and Marte of all Europe [6]

Andrew Boorde declares that

> the noble citie of London precelleth al other.[7]

---

[1] 1647. *London*, pp 2 and 3 (King Charles, his Augusta).
[2] See Johnston's *Place Names*, 1915.
[3] 1500–20 *Dunbar's Poems*, lxxxviij.
[4] 1594, I 1
[5] *Hesperides*, 1648.
[6] 1580 Lyly, *Euphues in London*.
[7] 1547. *Introduction of Knowledge*, chap. 1.

PRELUDE

and even Tusser, quitting for a moment his '500 points of good husbandry,' echoes the sentiment in his own way:

> Well London ! well thou bear'st the bell
> Of praise about, England throughout.[1]

In Harrington's 'Oceana' London is aptly portrayed:

The metropolitan or Capital City of 'Oceana' is commonly called Emporium[2];

and in a well-known satire:

> She is the great Bee-hive of Christendom,
> She is the Countryman's Laborinth.[3]

But in more serious vein, the reputed author of 'Eikon Basilike' addressed the Lord Mayor the year preceding the Restoration in impressive words not out of place after two and a half centuries:

For London (like Pallas) is furnished as with men of Counsel and Conduct, so with Treasure and Strength, with all sorts of arms and ammunition; being Camera Imperii Britanici, the Metropolis of the British Empire, a vast magazine of men and money, a nursery of all arts mechanick, Ingenuous and Military; a great entertainer of learning, and a noble Encourager of Religion; wanting nothing to make itself and the Nation happy if it have such heroick minds and honest hearts as become so rich, so great and so Christian a City.[4]

But as it is the outward aspect of the City that we are considering, let us recall the prospect that is given us in the old picture-maps of the 16th and 17th centuries, notably those by Van der Wyngaerde,[5] which shew the spire of the Cathedral at its full height, Visscher, Agas,[6] and Pieter Van den Keere in Norden's 'Speculum.'[7] Whether seen from the Bankside or, better still perhaps, from the tower

---

[1] 1575. *Biographical Verses.*
[2] 1656. (1887, pp. 197-8)
[3] 1632. Lupton's *London Carbonadoed*
[4] 1659. Dr. John Gauden, Bishop of Worcester.
[5] 1543.   [6] 1560   [7] 1593

xi

A LITERARY TOPOGRAPHY OF OLD LONDON

CHAPTER I

Royal Palaces

I

WESTMINSTER

THE ancient Palace of Westminster was the oldest of the palaces of our Kings, though the exact date of its foundation appears uncertain. A Parliamentary Broadside issued in 1647, being 'A Request for a Commission concerning the Palace of Westminster and Whitehall,' incidentally recites in brief its history down to Henry VIII.

> The Kings of England, times out of mind, were seized in fee of the Old Palace in Westminster till 28 Henry VIII, who then purchased a great Mansion House, parcell of the possession of the Archbishop of York near to the Palace of Westminster, which being decayed he built many fair lodgings and buildings for his pleasure and commodity.
> Henry VIII also seized in fee of St James' Park enclosed with a brick and stone wall, whereupon—28 Henry VIII—it was enacted by Parliament that all the Premises should be the King's whole Palace at Westminster and so to be called for ever [1]

The Palace was certainly in existence in Saxon times. Canute is said to have occupied it, and there is a tradition that the old story of his commanding the incoming tide to retire took place at Westminster on the shore of the river. It is told in 'Lestorie des Engles' of Geoffrey Gaimar (12th century) as happening 'pres del eglise ki Westmuster est apele.' The tide was disobedient, as we know:

> E plus e plus le flod montat.

[1] Broadside, B M., 816 m.g. (116).

A LITERARY TOPOGRAPHY OF OLD LONDON

Stow, on the authority of Ingulfus, writes:

> Next to the famous monastery is the King's principall Pallace, of what antiquity it is uncertain, but Edward the Confessor held his Court there, as may appeare by the testimony of sundrie . . . and for the most part remained there, where he ended his life and was buried in the Monastery which he had builded.[1]

William Fitz-Stephen, writing in the 12th century, gives an impression of its appearance:

> On the bank of the river the Royal Palace exalts its head and stretches wide. An incomparable structure furnished with bastions and a breastwork.[2]

William the Conqueror is said to have been crowned there and to have made additions to the original buildings. In the Bayeux Tapestry the Palace is depicted on the east side of the Abbey.[3]

The Great Hall was built by William Rufus c. 1097, the dimensions being, according to Stow, 270 feet by 74 feet, figures far beyond the requirements of an ordinary banqueting hall attached to a royal palace. but the early kings seem on special occasions to have entertained their subjects on a large scale. Geoffrey Gaimar, writing of William Rufus, says:

> A Westmoster sa feste tint
> En sa sale ki ert nouélé
> Tint une feste riche e bele

Kings, earls, and dukes were present, and 600 ushers at the doors indicated a multitude of visitors.[4] Stow tells us that Henry III commanded his treasurer to

> Cause 6000 poore people to be fed at Westminster . . the weake and aged to be placed in the great hall and in the lesser those that were most strong.

Its great size allowed space for men on horseback to enter, and a curious story is told of how King Edward II,

being at the celebration of the feast of Pentecost at dinner in the

---

[1] *Survey of London*, 1598 (1603, p. 466)
[2] *Description of London*, tr by S. Pegge, 1772, p. 25.
[3] See article by W R Lethaby in *Archæologia*, lx 146.
[4] *Lestorie des Engles*, Rolls Series, 5978

WESTMINSTER PALACE

open hall at Westminster a woman fantastically disguised entered on horsebacke and ryding about the table delivered him a letter, etc.[1]

The Palace is naturally the subject of continual reference in medieval records To quote only a few examples, in the reign of Edward III we hear of repair and learn, incidentally, where building stone was obtained. In the Calendar of Patent Rolls, March 3, 1350, we find:

> Appointment of Robert de Eshyngg to take workmen and stonemasons to dig stones in the Quarries of Abbotesbury co. Dorset and Bere co. Devon for some works at the Palace of Westminster.[2]

An architectural feature in the building must have been the tower which is alluded to in 15th century records, e.g. 'le toure' of the great palace of Westminster called 'le gatehouse' abutting in the palace on the east and towards the street called 'le Kyngstrete.' The gatehouse is constantly mentioned, as it was used as a prison.[3]

In Henry VII's time certain portions of the hall appeared to be divided off and allotted to the servants, e.g.

> Houses and dwelling places called 'Paradyse and Helle' in Westminster Hall . . . and a dwelling place called Purgatorie.[4]

What was termed the 'New Chamber' appeared to have been used as a place for any important state function, so in the reign of Edward III we read:

> The Chancellor delivered the great Seal for the government of England during the King's absence to the Bishop of Winchester the Treasurer in a Chamber called 'la Newe Chaumbre' in the Westminster Palace . . . to be kept in the Treasury.

The following extract records a national calamity:

> In this yere [1376] upon Trinite Soneday the viii day of Juyn withinne the Kynges Palys of Westm', deyde the noble flour of knighthood the good prince Edward [the Black Prince].[5]

There are indications of some additions in the reign

---
[1] Daniel's *History of England*, 1613 (1650, p. 210).
[2] *Calendar of Patent Rolls*, 23 Edward III.
[3] *Ibid* 16 Edward IV.　[4] *Calendar of Patent Rolls*, Nov. 5, 1503.
[5] *Chronicles of London*, 1089-1483.

of Henry IV in the shape of a new tower built specially for the benefit of the Queen Consort:

> Dec. 10, 1404. Grant for life to Joan Queen of England of a new Tower at the entrance of the great gate of the great hall within the palace of Westminster ... for the arrangement of her Charters etc.[1]

In another record only a few years earlier (1371) we find mention of some of the expenses of upkeep, e.g.

> Richard de Sutton keeper of the King's Private Palace was granted 6d. per day for life. The King's head gardener 12d. per day.[2]

In 1460 Henry VI was kept a prisoner in his own palace, as William Gregory relates in his contemporary chronicle:

> Soo he [the Duke of York] rode forthe unto Lundon tylle he come to Westemyster to Kyng Harrys palys and there he claymyde the crowne of Inglonde and he kepte Kyng Harry there by fors and strengyth tylle at the laste the Kyng for fere of dethe grantyd hym the Crowne [3]

Yet Stow writes of two destructions by fire, one in 1290, the other in 1512. Doubtless he means injury or partial destruction.[4] As to the fire in 1512 he adds:

> Since which time it hath not been re-edified, only the great Hall which serveth as afore for feastes at coronations.[5]

Executions took place there in the Old Palace Yard. There the gunpowder conspirators met their doom, as Walter Young describes in his Diary (January 31, 1605-6).[6] Thirteen years later on a much sadder occasion Sir Walter Raleigh met his fate with a noble fortitude—the last tragic scene in a career clouded by misfortune yet not inglorious:

> The next morning betweene the Sheriffs of Middlesex Sir Walter Rawleigh was brought to the old Palace in Westminster where a large scaffold was erected for the execution.[7]

---

[1] *Calendar of Patent Rolls*, 6 Henry IV, vol ii. 473.
[2] *Pell Records*, 44 Edward III. [3] *Op. cit.* Camden Society, p 208.
[4] In recent years, during structural alterations some portions of the Norman work of Rufus have been traced, viz. some buttresses on the west side of the great hall. See article by W. R. Lethaby in *Archæologia*, lx.
[5] *Survey of London*, 1603, pp. 460, 471. [6] Camden Society, p. 2.
[7] 1618. *Proceedings against Sir Walter Rawley at the King's Bench-Barre*, 1648, p. 27.

WESTMINSTER PALACE

There were smaller halls which in time came to be used mostly for legal purposes. The largest of these,[1] known as the 'White Hall,'[2] was, so Stow says, in his time used as the Court of Wards and Liveries. One of the most ancient apartments was that known as 'The Painted Chamber.' Of this Camden says:

> Knowen by the name of St. Edwards painted chamber because the tradition holdeth that the said King Edward there died.[3]

Old plates shew a long apartment badly lighted by small windows in deep embrasures, the walls covered with tapestry. Said to date from the time of the Confessor.[4] One of the closing scenes in the tragedy of King Charles's trial and execution took place in this chamber. After the Restoration Evelyn witnessed a curious ceremony here:

> To London and saw the bathing and rest of the ceremonies of the Knights of the Bath preparatory to the Coronation; it was in the Painted Chamber Westminster. I might have received this honour but declined it.[5]

In earlier times the ceremony took place at the Tower.

The old Clochard or Bell Tower, which was an appanage of St. Stephen's Chapel, stood in very nearly the position of the present Clock Tower. It was built in 1365-6 by Edward III, with whom the old Palace was a favourite residence, and was much improved by him. The Tower was built of stone and timber covered with lead, and had three bells.[6] Of these bells there was a tradition, so Stow says, that 'their ringing sowred all the drinke in the towne.' Their weight was over-estimated. An inscription ran:

> King Edward made me,
> Thirtie thousand and three
> Take me downe and wey me,
> And more shall ye find me.

[1] See Chapter V. on the Parliament Houses.
[2] In early days '*la Blanche Chaumbre*, upon the River Thames'—*Cal of Close Rolls*, April 28, 1340.
[3] *Britannia* (Holland's tr), 1610, p 431.
[4] See Smith's *Antiquities of Westminster*
[5] *Diary*, April 19, 1661
[6] See *Archæologia*, vol. xxxvii. 23

A LITERARY TOPOGRAPHY OF OLD LONDON

But when taken down—so Stow says—the three together did not weigh so much as this.[1]

Hollar's view of Westminster Hall shews a large open space in front of the principal entrance, and on the other side of this a lofty square-built clock-tower. This would seem to be the Tower mentioned by Stow,[2] 'containing a Clock which striketh every houre on a great Bell ... in a calme will be heard into the Citie of London.'

Michael Drayton, whose favourite topic in 'Polyolbion' was the beauty of rivers and riverside objects, was impressed with the prospect of the old Palace and the Abbey which with St. Stephen's Chapel and many other buildings and towers formed a group which, seen from the river or the opposite bank, must have been unrivalled.

> Then Westminster the next great Tames does entertain
> That vaunts her Palace large and her most sumptuous Fane.[3]

The old Palace and its *entourage* remained, subject to certain changes, till its destruction by fire in 1833; only the Great Hall was spared and is still with us. The west side of it was much defaced when the various Law Courts were added.

It is worth remembering that Chaucer held the post of Clerk of the Works to the old Palace, and his house is said to have been near where Henry the Seventh's Chapel was afterwards built.

---

[1] Stow's *Survey*, 1603, p. 474. Mr. Kingsford, in a note in his edition of Stow, says that it was another Bell Tower, not this one, which belonged to St. Stephen's Chapel.

[2] *Survey*, 1603, p 475. In the *Calendar of Patent Rolls*, Richard II, Part II, mention is made of the custody of the Great Clock (1377 and 1378). Confirmed 1399. Granted to John Pakynton for life for keeping of the clock within the Palace of Westminster. But an entry, Dec 22, 1395, records a grant to William Wodeward, 'foundur,' with wages of 6d. a day on condition that he repair it at his own expense. Then described as 'the great clock within the Palace of Westminster.' Hollar's view of the old Palace Yard may be seen in Jesse's *London*, vol. i. The conduit is a prominent erection.

[3] 1622. *Polyolbion*, xvii. 89 The Land's Tribunal Seat he calls the Palace, but this aspect is dealt with in another chapter.

II

WHITEHALL

As mentioned elsewhere,[1] Henry VIII added very largely to the Archiepiscopal Palace originally known as Whitehall and now reassuming that title, and many new buildings were erected on the St. James's Park side of the road, there being also built two fine arched gateways, the northern one of which was said to have been designed by Holbein This was a good example of Tudor work and comprised a massive and lofty tower somewhat in the style of Hampton Court,[2] flanked by two smaller octagonal towers. Pennant says 'built of glazed and coloured brick,' but a later writer has it 'built of small square stones and flint boulders'[3] Hollar's view (1680) shews this gate at right angles to the Banqueting Hall of Inigo Jones, to which allusion will be made later, the space between being occupied by smaller buildings with four gables.

Queen Elizabeth made some additions to Whitehall in the form of a Banqueting House,[4] but it was not of a very substantial character and did not last many years. The Queen rather favoured Greenwich Palace, the place of her birth, but her funeral was at Whitehall. Dekker has some rhymes

> Greenwich for her birth
> Richmond for her death
> White-hall for her Funerall
>
> The Queen was brought by Water to Whitehall:
> At every stroake the oares teares let fall :
> More clung about the barge Fish under water
> Wept out their eyes of pearle and swam blind after.
> I think the Barge-men might with easier thyes
> Have rowde her thither in her peoples eyes !
> For howsoe're, thus much my thoughts have skan'd,
> S'had come by water had she come by land.[5]

---

[1] See 'Bishops' Palaces'
[2] There is a good drawing of this by Silvestre (1640).
[3] See Smith's *Antiquities of Westminster*
[4] This is alluded to in the *Acts of the Privy Council* (1587, vol xv. p 287). 'Their Lordships sate in Counsell in the little banketing house in the garden'
[5] *The Wonderful Yeare*, 1603

A LITERARY TOPOGRAPHY OF OLD LONDON

James I rebuilt the Banqueting House of Queen Elizabeth somewhere about 1607. So we read in 'Camden's Annals.' But it was burnt down a few years after. Sir Richard Baker does not credit King James with much building of importance:

> Structures of piety King James made none at all, not many of magnificence, only the great Banketing House at White-Hall.[1]

This alludes to the Banqueting Hall designed by Inigo Jones and decorated by Rubens, which is the only portion of Whitehall which remains to this day. It was part of a large scheme of rebuilding projected by the great architect of the period but not carried out.

In the early years of the reign of Charles I there were many festivities at Whitehall. Masques were frequent, many being the composition of Ben Jonson, the elaborate and fanciful designs and scenery being the work of Inigo Jones. 'Albion's Triumph' was the title of a masque by Townsend.

> The King and the Maskers dance the mayne maske. . . . The scene is varied into a landscapt in which was a prospect of the Kings Pallace of Whitehall and part of the Citie of London.[2]

This was acted by King Charles and his Lords 'the Sunday after Twelfe Night, 1631.' On the following Shrove Tuesday another masque, 'Tempe restord,' was 'presented by the Queene and fourteene ladies.'

In 1641 there was a Royal wedding.

> May 2. The Prince of Orange (who had tarried here ever since the 20th of April) married the Princess Mary at Whitehall with all the solemnities appertaining to the ceremony.[3]

But the troubles were beginning. The same year the King writes:

> that the late tumult had caused him to fortifie White-Hall for the security of his own Person.[4]

---

[1] *Chronicle*, 1643, 'James I,' p 150
[2] 1631. A. Townsend, *Albion's Triumph*, p 16.
[3] 1665. Baker's *Chron continued*, p 532.
[4] *Ibid* 547.

WHITEHALL

Shortly after a Ballad of the day indicates the state of affairs, but not with despondency:

> Though for a time we see Whitehall
> With cobweb hangings on the wall
> Instead of gold and silver brave
> Which formerly 'twas wont to have.
>
> . . . . .
>
> Which again shall be when the time you see
> That the King enjoys his own again.[1]

But the King did not enjoy his own again, and the last tragic scene took place in front of the great Banqueting Hall, the scene of so many happy festivities. These are the concluding words of the Death Warrant:

> These are therefore to will and require you to see the said sentence executed in the open street before Whitehall with full effect

The King was led to the scaffold through one of the windows of the Hall or an opening purposely made:

> A guard was made all along the Galleries and the Banqueting House but behind the Soldiers abundance of men and women crowded in . . . And as his Majesty passed by with a cheerful look, heard them pray for him, the soldiers not rebuking . . There was a passage broken through the wall by which the King pass'd unto the scaffold[2]

It was a political enemy who thus testified to the calm dignity with which the King met his fate:

> He nothing common did or mean
> Upon that memorable scene
>
> . . . . .
>
> Nor called the gods with vulgar spite
> To vindicate his helpless right[3]

Five years after we hear of Cromwell, newly dignified as 'Lord Protector,' appearing at Whitehall. In a letter addressed to Lady Hatton we read:

> Whitehall is making very fyne to interteyne the newe Protector, and that he and his lady tooke the places, I meane the closett, looking into the Chaple . . . wch formerly were used by the King and lately by the Queenes retinewe[4]

---
[1] c 1643, attributed to Martin Parker
[2] 1648–9. Sir Thos Herbert, *Memoirs of King Charles I* (1702, p 133).
[3] Andrew Marvell, *Horatian Ode* (c. 1657).
[4] 1653–4 Camden Soc, *Hatton Letters*, 10

A LITERARY TOPOGRAPHY OF OLD LONDON

During the Civil War it would seem that the wages of the porter at Whitehall were unpaid. His petition is on record:

> March 22, 1653-4 Stephen Sayers, porter at Whitehall to the Protector for satisfaction for disbursements and 8 years service He stated that he had served 6 years at Whitehall and 2 at Somerset House . . . provided fire, candles etc. spending 166*l*.[1]

The Palace of Whitehall must have largely increased in size during the reigns of the first three Stuart Kings, though there was no large and dignified building of uniform design on the scale of the Banqueting Hall. A ground-plan of the Palace made by Fisher in the reign of Charles II shews something like a small town of suites of apartments extending along the river front from Whitehall stairs to Scotland Yard, and also on the west side of what is now the street called 'Whitehall.' A Hall is shewn and a Chapel[2] There had been a library at all events from the time of Elizabeth, but probably earlier; some of the books may have belonged to Cardinal Wolsey. When Sir Thomas Bodley was forming the Library at Oxford which was opened in 1603, he wrote to Dr. Thomas James, who was assisting him

> I would have us lay our ground-sells sure. and therefore will gather all our manuscripts first I do not doubt, but we shall find a great many in White-hall Library.[3]

In another letter he writes:

> I have gotten the warrant from the King under his hand and privy seal for the choice of any books that I shall like (Letter cx.).

The following quotation from a play shews that the galleries at Whitehall were at a later date a place of public resort:

> Observe but any morning what people do when they get together on the Exchange, in Westminster Hall, or the galleries in Whitehall.[4]

---

[1] *State Papers Domestic*, vol lxviii p 45
[2] See Smith's *Antiquities of Westminster.*
[3] *Remains* (1703), Letter 217
[4] Wycherley, *The Plain Dealer* (c 1667), I i

WHITEHALL

We are even told that a pickpocket was bold enough to exercise his skill when mixing with the crowd in the presence-chamber, and that King James I, our British Solomon, exercised summary justice, not wisely or legally though effectually:

> A cut-purse being taken in the presence, King James commanded the Lord Garnet, the Knight Marshal, presently to hang the Cut-purse, which was done instantly; but the Knight Marshall was fain to get a pardon under seal.[1]

The following is the impression of an outsider in the time of Charles II.

> The Thames washed the sides of a large, though not magnificent palace of the Kings of Great Britain; from the stairs of this Palace the Court used to take water in the summer evenings [2]

Cowley, the popular poet of the Restoration period, calls it

> the White Palace where the King does reign
> Who lays his Laws and bridges o'er the main;

a statement less correct than complimentary to the King and the Navy.[3] Thomas Fuller gives his impression of the Palace in his own way:

> A good Hypocrite, promising less than it performeth and more convenient within then comely without, to which the nursery of Saint James's was an appendant.[4]

Cromwell's two daughters were married here, so Clarendon relates:

> These marriages were celebrated at White-Hall with all imaginable pomp and lustre; and . . . though the marriages were performed . according to the Rites and ceremonies then in use, they were presently afterwards in private married by Ministers ordained by Bishops and according to the form in the Book of Common Prayer; and this with the privity of Cromwell [5]

---

[1] 1652 Sir Edward Peyton, 'Divine Catastrophe,' *Secret History of the Court of James I*, ii. 433
[2] Count Ant. Hamilton, *Grammont Memoirs* (1853), p 146
[3] *Works* (1680), p. 26
[4] *Worthies of England* (1662), ii. 235
[5] 1670 *History of the Rebellion* (1798), B. xv. 212.

A LITERARY TOPOGRAPHY OF OLD LONDON

The old Cockpit, built by Henry VIII, and at one time a private Play-house, was superseded by or converted into, a residence, and was occupied for a time by Cromwell

> He removed from the Cockpit which house the Parliament had assigned him to take possession of White-hall which he assigned to himself His wife seemed at first unwilling to remove thither tho afterwards she became better satisfied with her grandeur [1]

Lord Pembroke seems to have had the use of the house in the late King's time, for he writes to Edward Hyde and dates his letter from 'The Cockpit, June 30, 1642.'[2] In the year after the Restoration the Duke of Albemarle had it, and Pepys was there and saw a play.

> 20 April 1661. Saw 'The humorous Lieutenant'[3] acted before the King

Two years after there is another entry in the Diary:

> Nov 9, 1663 The Duke of Monmouth is to have part of the Cockpit now built for lodgings for him

The ground-plan of Whitehall Palace prepared by John Fisher has already been alluded to.[4] At the east end of the long river frontage we see 'Whitehall Palace Stairs,' and near by what is called 'The Great Hall' and 'The Chapel.' Then we see the large inner court with a vast number of 'lodgings' and offices and so approach the great Banqueting Hall from the back. Regarding this from the open space in front (now the street which we call 'Whitehall'), we see the main entrance to the palace on our left, and on the right, at right angles to the Banqueting Hall, the Holbein Gate which appeared to serve as a crossing place to St. James's Palace on the opposite side. Here among a multiplicity of buildings we see the Tennis Court, the Tilt Yard and the 'Cockpit,' which last is shewn as being octagonal in plan. At the west end of the river front we see the Privy Garden and steps and beyond a spacious

---

[1] 1654. *Memoirs of Edmund Ludlow* (1894), 1 379
[2] *Clarendon State Papers*
[3] By Fletcher.
[4] Published 1747. A copy at British Museum

ST. JAMES'S PALACE

Bowling Green stretching from King Street to the river. The 'Stone Gallery' is shewn on the south side of the Privy Garden. In the gardens was much fine statuary wilfully destroyed in 1659 by a cook living near by who

in sermon time with a smith's great hamer brake there those goodly statues of brass and marble the best workmanship in Europe [1]

III

St. James's Palace

St. James's Palace, already mentioned, occupied the site of an ancient Leper House known as St James's Hospital and founded probably in Norman times—Stow says ' before the time of any man's memory.' It was dedicated to St. James-the-Less, Bishop of Jerusalem,

for fourteen sisters, maidens that were leprous, living chastly and honestly in divine service.

The sisterhood, as one source of income, had rights to receive the profits of an Annual Fair held on the Eve of St. James's Day. The Fair was the forerunner, so it is said, of the ' May Fair ' which in after years gave a name to the district so called.

Stow speaks of the Palace built by Henry VIII on the site of the Leper Hospital as a ' goodly manor,' [2] intended, with the Park, to be an adjunct to Whitehall. There is reference, however, to a Palace of St. James at Westminster at a much earlier period than the reign of Henry VIII, for there is an allusion to such a Palace, in conjunction with other minor Royal Palaces, as being in official use in the reign of Henry VI.

The Counsell began first at Eltham and than it removed to Schene and fro thens vnto Mortlake and from thense to Seynt James beside Westmynster.[3]

---

[1] T. Rugge, *A Collection of Material Occurrences*, Brit. Mus. Addit. MSS., printed in *Gent. Mag*, 1852, part 1 pp 477-9
[2] Stow's *Survey* (1603), pp. 106, 455.
[3] *Chronicles of London* (Cotton MSS, Cleopatra, C IV, 1437-9).

A LITERARY TOPOGRAPHY OF OLD LONDON

One can hardly imagine the Council meeting at a leper house.

At the time of its transfer to the King, the Hospital with a large area of land was in the possession of Eton College; the deed conveying the property to the Crown has been preserved, and the substance of it is printed in 'Letters and Papers of Henry VIII'[1]:

> Indenture made 5 Sept 23 Henry VIII between the King and Roger Lupton, Provost of Eton College, covenanting that the King shall have the site etc. of the house of S. James in the Field with 185½ acres between Charing Cross and Aye Hill.

There were other outlying pieces of land included.

In exchange the College was to receive the Manor of Baudewyn's, Dertford, Kent, with other manorial property: also the advowsons of Newington, Kent, and Ghatesham, Suffolk. These properties came into the hands of the King either by the suppression of the monastic houses or in consequence of the attainder of Cardinal Wolsey.[2]

The new Palace was a good specimen of the Tudor architecture of the period, of brick and somewhat in the style of Hampton Court, though on a much smaller scale. The main gateway entrance was through a square tower having octagonal corner turrets. The building as we see it now is almost entirely of a later period. Henry lived there during the life of his second wife, and the chimney-piece of the Presence Chamber bore the initials of the King and Anne Boleyn. The Chapel Royal was famous for its choir, and the 'Children of the Chapel' acquired some fame as actors in the Mystery Plays which prevailed in the time of Henry VIII, and in the next century became a company of actors well known on the stage in legitimate drama.

Queen Mary took up her residence at St. James's, and it was known as her 'Manor House.' At the time of Wyatt's rebellion she was living there.

> He (Wyatt) and his Mates ranne downe, underneth yᵉ parke wal of bricke adioynynge to the Queenes Manor house called Sainct James . . untyll he came to Charinge Crosse.[3]

[1] Vol v p 201
[3] 1555. J. Procter, *Wyates rebellion*, fol 69.
[2] *Ibid.* p. 288.

ST. JAMES'S PALACE

It was here that the Queen died:

> It is to be remembered that the said Princes departed out of this transsytory Lyffe and World .. in the vjth yere of her Highnes Reigne at her Manner of St. James beyond the Charynge Crosse[1];

and Fabyan in his 'Chronicle' adds:

> where she hadde lien sicke long before of a quarteine feuer.[2]

In 1638 Charles I gave the use of the Palace to Marie de Medici, the Queen's mother, who was received in London with some state and a procession, though there had been tumults at her landing. Edmund Waller, in his usual courtly style, wrote a panegyric:

> Great Queen of Europe! where thy off-spring wears
> All the chief crowns; where Princes are thy heirs;
> As welcome thou to sea-girt Britains shore
> As erst Latona (who fair Cynthia bore)
> To Delos was.[3]

But the Queen Mother was not in sympathy with the English people, and she returned to France after three years.

Before the Civil War we hear of expensive additions, seemingly some new building in the Park:

> The City of London was invited to a loan but refused and pleaded poverty . . . yet the Citizens were content to offer an ample sum towards the building of a magnificent Palace for the King's Court in St. James's Park according to Inigo Jones's modell (1640).[4]

It was at St. James's Palace that Charles I took farewell of his children, and here he spent the last night of his life.

After the King's execution the young Duke of York, afterwards James II, was in the charge of the Parliament and placed in St. James's Palace, being then fifteen years old. By the help of friends he managed to escape:

> The Duke of York, disguised in Women's apparel, made his escape from St. James's by water, and landed at Dort in Holland, by the help of one Col. Bampfield sent over purposely on that design by the Queen.[5]

---

[1] C. 1558. Leland, *Miscell. Pieces from Orig. MS*, vol. v. p. 308.
[2] 1559, ii. 566.   [3] 1638. 'To the Queen Mother of France.'
[4] Baker's *Chron* 'Charles I.' (1665), p. 512.
[5] Baker's *Chron*., continued by Phillips (1665), p. 604.

A LITERARY TOPOGRAPHY OF OLD LONDON

There was a library at the Palace, of which Cromwell took possession, and from it, it would seem, he gave duplicates to his friends.

> To the Keeper of the Library of St James's. These are to will and require you . . . to deliver unto Sir Oliver Fleming . . . two or three such books as he shall choose, of which there is a double copy in the Library.[1]

It was here, in 1677, that Mary, the daughter of James, Duke of York, by his first wife, Anne Hyde, the daughter of the future Lord Clarendon, was married to William, Prince of Orange.

IV

SOMERSET HOUSE

The original Somerset House in the Strand has long since passed away, but it occupied the site of the Somerset House still standing, though very different in appearance and design. It was not built for a Royal Palace but designed for the residence of the Duke of Somerset who, as Protector of the young King Edward VI, made use of his position to acquire great wealth and assumed the rôle of an autocrat. To provide materials for his monster palace he disregarded the rights of owners whether private or ecclesiastical. The houses of the Bishops of Chester (or Lichfield) and Worcester were demolished, as was the beautiful cloister on the north side of St. Paul's and the greater part of the Priory Church of St. John, Clerkenwell. The buildings, said to have been designed by John of Padua, were commenced in the first year of his Protectorship but were never finished, as Somerset was executed in 1552. It then became Crown property, and was in some way completed, though not on the scale intended by the founder. In Queen Mary's reign it was occupied by her sister Elizabeth, whose residence there is noted in Machyn's Diary :

> The xxviij Nov 1556 came ryding thrugh Fletstrett unto Somerset Place my good lade Elizabeth's grace the quen's syster.

[1] Order of O. Cromwell, 1649 (1871), Carlyle, ii. 102.

SOMERSET HOUSE

... The iij day of Desember' cam ryding from her plasse my lade Elizabeth's grace from Somersett place down Fletstrett ... and so her grace toke her way toward Bysshope Atfield plasse (Hatfield House).[1]

Harrison, the author of 'A Description of Britaine,' has a good word for Somerset and a note of regret that he did not live to finish his Palace:

Of Somerset Place I speak not, yet if the first beginner thereof (I mean the Lord Edward the learned and godly Duke of Somerset) had lived, I doubt not that it should have been well finished and brought to a sumptuous end.[2]

Elizabeth as Queen lived rather a gayer life than as Princess, and we hear of plays at Somerset House:

An Antick Playe and a Comodye shewed presented and enacted before her highnes on Shroue tewsdaie at night at Somerset place by her maiesties servauntes.[3]

Henslowe, no doubt, was engaged in the production of plays at Somerset House, for we note in his Diary an entry in 1594:

Layd owt for gowinge and cominge to Somerset howe(s) for iiij tymes .. 1s 4d[4]

In the reigns of the first two Stuart Kings dramatic entertainments, frequently masques, were much in vogue at Somerset House, and favoured by the Queen Consorts, who often personally took part. In 1626 we find the French Ambassador visiting Queen Henrietta Maria in order to view the Lord Mayor's Show on the river, a sight, doubtless, new to both of them:

Next day Monday the 9th (November) which is the election of the Mayor I came in the morning to Sommerset House to meet the queen who had come there to see him go on the Thames on his way to Westminster to be sworn in.[5]

When the Princess Marie Henriette married Charles I and became anglicised into Queen Henrietta Maria, she

---
[1] 1560-3. Machyn's *Diary*, p. 120.
[2] In Holinshed's *Chronicle* (1577), Book II c. 9.
[3] 1584. *Revels Accounts, Audit Office*, Rd. 1213, Revels No. 10 (Feuillerat, *Revels Office*).
[4] *Dulwich College MSS.*, no. vii. (Cat p. 158).
[5] Marshall de Bassompierre, *Embassy in England* (tr. 1819).

brought with her a number of her French retainers, who were settled at Somerset House. All would have been well had not the French servants adopted insolent manners which became unbearable. The King intervened, and his speech to the servants on July 1, 1626, has been preserved

> Gentlemen and Ladies, I am driven to that extremity, as I am personally come to acquaint you that I very earnestly desire your return into France.[1]

This dismissal was one cause of the after rupture with France.

In the Queen's marriage contract with Charles it was agreed that she was to have the free use of her own religion, and she was allowed to bring over a number of Capuchin priests who were accommodated at Somerset House, and a new chapel designed by Inigo Jones was erected. This was commonly resorted to by Roman Catholics in London As Clarendon tells us[2]:

> The Papists had for many years enjoy'd a great calm . . they resorted at common hours to Mass to Somerset House and returned thence in great multitudes.

Moreover complaints were made that the Queen's Capuchin Friars were very active in perverting the King's subjects from the true religion. The House of Commons therefore passed a motion

> Humbly to desire her Majesty that the said Friers may be kept in and not suffered to go abroad to pervert the people and draw them to be reconciled to the Church of Rome (1641).[3]

But when the troubles began and Charles was no longer in London, the Puritanism of the powers in authority caused summary action, and the Capuchins were expelled and sent back to France. This gave the King great offence, and he wrote in 1643

> To our trusty and welbeloued Richard Browne our Resident with our deere Brother the French King.

---

[1] 'To the French servants of the Queen at Somerset House,' *Works of Charles I* (1662), p. 364.
[2] C 1647 *Hist of the Rebellion* (1798), vol 1 Book 11. 255.
[3] J Nalson, *Collection of Affairs of State* (1683), 11. 445

SOMERSET HOUSE

> Wee beleeve that before this letter the Capuchins of Somersett house, or some from there, will be arrived at Paris and have represented there how disgracefully they were lately entreated at London. Wee are exceedingly displeased that soe high an affront hath been put upon the Treaty between vs and the French King our Brother.[1]

A few years later, while the King was still living, but helpless:

> Under pretence of searching for arms and taking away superstitious Pictures, they caused the Queen's Chapel at Somerset House . . . to be most licentiously rifled.[2]

Evelyn describes the regal pomp of Oliver Cromwell's funeral:

> Saw ye superb funerall of ye Protector. He was carried from Somerset House in a velvet bed of state drawn by six horses houss'd with ye same, the pall held by his new Lords, Oliver lying in effigie in royal robes and crown'd with a crown, sceptre and globe, like a King.[3]

Cowley was present, though with some reluctance, and wrote his reflections:

> I found there had been much more cost bestowed than either the dead man, or indeed death itself could deserve . . . the whole was so managed that, methought it somewhat represented the life of him for whom it was made; much noise, much tumult, much expense, much magnificence, much vain-glory, briefly, a great show, and yet after all this but an ill sight.[4]

At the Restoration, on her return from exile, Queen Henrietta Maria took up her residence at Somerset House. Waller, as was his wont, was ready with verses:

> Great Queen that does our Island bless
> With Princes and with Palaces,
> Treated so ill, chased from your throne
> Returning you adorn the town.

Waller's memory must have been bad, otherwise it would have occurred to him that about six years before, in a Eulogy on Cromwell, he had said:

> Let partial spirits, still aloud complain
> Think themselves injured that they cannot reign.

---
[1] Cited by J. Evelyn, *Works* (1879), iv. 234
[2] Clarendon's *Rebellion*, c. 1647 (1798), vol. vi. Book vii. 20.
[3] *Diary*, 22 Oct. 1658
[4] *A Discourse on the Government of Oliver Cromwell*, p. 130

A LITERARY TOPOGRAPHY OF OLD LONDON

Referring to the Queen's new buildings:

> Can such a pile from ruin rise?
> This, like the first Creation, shews
> As if at your command it rose.[1]

Waller's verses indicate that considerable damage must have been done during the Protectorate. No doubt the Chapel of Inigo Jones suffered severely.

Abraham Cowley wrote verses on the same subject in 1663. The house is supposed to be telling its own story:

> my front looks down
> On all the pride and business of the town;
> My other Fair and more majestic face
> .   .   .
> For ever gazes on itself below;
> In the best mirror that the world can show.[2]

In the painting of the Thames ascribed to Cornelius Bol, a Flemish artist, at the Dulwich Gallery, Somerset House is prominent. The house has a long front to the river relieved by battlemented towers, the centre one having a cupola. The detail is in the late Gothic style. Apparently this was painted before the additions and the Chapel of Inigo Jones. There is a river-gate and wall and broad steps for landing.[3]

A visitor in 1664 gives his impression of the Chapel:

> Feb. 28. It being Sunday, I went to the Queen Mother's Chapell which is a stately one, well painted and adorned with a large gold crucifix ... tapers, lamps and the like.[4]

John Evelyn, who always had a critical eye for trees, and who as the author of 'Sylva' speaks with some

---

[1] E. Waller, *Upon Her Majesty's New Buildings at Somerset House*
[2] *Repairing Somerset House* (ed. 1680, p. 26).
[3] A model, shewing the house as it appeared in 1650, has been made by James P Maginnis, from drawings prepared by Walter H. Godfrey. The river front has the most imposing appearance. The Strand side having a smaller frontage gives the building a somewhat one-sided appearance.
[4] *Journal of E. Browne*, 1664 (1836, p. 51).

SOMERSET HOUSE

authority, notes that the French priests in the last reign left a reminder of their brief stay by planting elms:

> There was a cloyster of the right French Elm in the little Garden near to Her Majesty's the Queen Mother's Chappel at Somersethouse which were (I suppose) planted there by the F. Capuchines.[1]

During the reign of James I. the place was called 'Denmark House' in honour of Queen Anne, and partly, perhaps, as a compliment to the King of Denmark, her father, when he paid a visit to London. It was the Queen's favourite Palace, and her body lay there before its interment in the Abbey:

> Queen Anne died at Hampton Court whose corps was brought to Denmark House and from thence conveighed to Westminster.[2]

This was in 1619, but the name was still used, for three years afterwards in the 'Diary of Walter Yonge' we read:

> April 1622. The Emperor's Ambassador came to London and was received and entertained in Westminster Hall with great pomp . . . He lieth in Denmark House, or Somerset House.[3]

When James I died

> at Denmark House the hall there was made a Chappell for the tyme, where the Confessor read Morning prayer daylie. . . .
> King Charles was him selfe in persone the Cheife mourner and followed the corps of his father on foote from Denmark House unto Westminster Church.[4]

There was, one hundred years earlier than this, another house in the eastern part of the City in Fenchurch Street, called Denmark House, and, strange to say, we are told of another foreign ambassador who was lodged there. Pennant tells us (on the authority of Holinshed) that an ambassador was sent in 1557 'from the Emperor of Cathaie, Muscovia and Russeland.'[5]

---

[1] 1664. *Silva* (1729), p. 43
[2] Baker's *Chronicle*, 'James I' (1643), p 143
[3] *Diary of Walter Yonge*, Camden Society, p. 55.
[4] 1625 Order of the Funerall of Kinge James, *The Old Cheque Book*, Camden Soc., 1872.
[5] The visit was said to be in consequence of the new discovery of the White Sea by Chancellor.

A LITERARY TOPOGRAPHY OF OLD LONDON

V

BRIDEWELL PALACE

A holy well was attached to the Church of St Bride or Bridget in Fleet Street, but the virtues of the well did not extinguish the fire that destroyed the Church. The well, if existing, is no longer available either to work miracles or for the uses of common life, but its existence in early days gave a name to Bridewell, sometime famous as a Palace, though having, perhaps, a wider notoriety as a hospital and a prison.[1]

The ancient Palace that occupied the site adjacent was, according to Pennant, built partly out of the remains of the old castle, the western *Arx Palatina* of the City which stood near the Fleet. In 1087 William the Conqueror used some of the stones for the rebuilding of St. Paul's, destroyed by fire in that year, but the place was left sufficiently habitable for some of our early Kings to make use of it. Some centuries later Cardinal Wolsey lived there for a time. As his biographer says, he

behaved himself so politickly that he was made one of the King's Privie Councell and increased in favour daily, to whom he gave a house at Bridewell neer Flete-stret where he kept house for his family.[2]

In the year 1513 Wolsey, writing to the Lord Admiral, with directions as to naval matters, dates his letter ' June 6 : At my poor house at the Bridewell.'[3]

In the year 1522, in preparation for the visit of the Emperor Charles V, Henry 'builded there a stately and beautifull house of new,' so Stow tells us, and Pennant adds that it was erected in six weeks. But the Emperor did not himself occupy the new Palace, leaving it to the use of his nobles, while he himself was lodged at the Blackfriars

---

[1] Some fragments of a pump may still be seen and mark the position of the well.

[2] *Negotiations of Thomas Wolsey, composed by one of his own Servants* (Cavendish), 1641, p 48

[3] *State Papers Domestic*, 5 Henry VIII.

BRIDEWELL PALACE

situate on the opposite side of the river Fleet, ' a gallery being made out of the house over the water and through the Wall of the Cittie into the Emperour's lodging.' An engraving of 1540 shews the Palace having a castellated front to the river with three bastions and a range of buildings behind. Here in 1529 Henry and Queen Katherine of Arragon were lodged while the great question of the Divorce was under discussion at the Blackfriars—so Stow says—by Cardinal Campeius, the Pope's Legate, and Wolsey; but Fuller says this took place at Bridewell:

> Cardinal Campeius and Wolsey, in their court at Bridewell wherein the divorce was judiciously handled, intended only to produce a solemn nothing, their court being but the clock set according to the dial of Rome and the instructions received thence.[1]

In Shakespeare's great scene[2] in the play, late editions give the place of the Court as ' in the Hall of Blackfriars,' but the folio of 1623 does not mention the exact locality. Cavendish speaks of ' a certain place in the Blackfriars.' This is his comment

> It was by the council determined that the King and the Queen his wife should be lodged at Bridewell and that in the Blackfriars a certain place should be appointed where the King and the Queen might most conveniently repair to the Court, there to be erected . . which was the strangest and newest sight and device that ever was read or heard in any history or chronicle in any region; that a King and a Queen should be convented and constrained by process compellatory to appear in any Court as common persons[3]

VI

THE SAVOY

The Savoy Palace took its name from Peter, Earl of Savoy and Richmond, who is reputed to have built it about 1245, but according to Pennant ' the palace of the potent Simon de Montford, earl of Leicester, stood on this place,' and Henry III granted it to Peter of Savoy, uncle

---

[1] Thos. Fuller, *The Holy State*, 1642 (1840, p. 206).
[2] *Henry VIII*, II iv
[3] Cavendish, *Life of Wolsey*, a 1562 (1885, p 113).

A LITERARY TOPOGRAPHY OF OLD LONDON

to his Queen Eleanor, and he bestowed it on the fraternity of Mountjoy. Queen Eleanor purchased it for her son Edmund, Earl of Lancaster, whose son Henry,[1] coming into possession, entirely rebuilt it. In the reign of Edward III, after the battle of Poictiers, King John of France, being a prisoner, returned to England with Edward the Black Prince, being treated more as a friend than a prisoner, and was lodged at the Savoy Palace, where he remained for five years, and was then allowed to return to France. Shortly afterwards he returned to England on a visit, and had the use of Savoy Palace as a guest, and—to quote Fabyan's ' Chronicle ' :

> Whyle the sayde Kynge John laye at the sayd place of Savoy about the begynnynge of March folowynge a greuvus sykenesse toke hym of the which he dyed the viij daye of Apryll (1362) [2]

At the time of the rebellion under Wat Tyler and Jack Straw (1381), John of Gaunt held the Savoy. He was specially obnoxious to the rebels, as alluded to in several early chronicles, e.g. :

> This yere (4 Richard II) the comones of Essex and Kent . . . brenden the Dukes Place of Lancastre called Saveye and wolde fayn an had the Duke of Lancastre, but as grace was he myghte not be founden [3]

and in Hardyng's ' Chronicle ' (1543) :

> The Cômons brent the Sauoye a place fayre
> For eiuill wyll they had unto duke John.

A contemporary ballad indicates that the destruction was complete :

> Savoy semely sett
> *heu ! funditus igne cadebat.*[4]

At the time of Jack Cade's rebellion in the reign of

---

[1] Henry Plantagenet, the first Duke of Lancaster.
[2] 1516. Fabyan's *Chron* , fol cxvj.
[3] Nicholas' *Chron.*, p. 73 (from 15 cent. MS. Harleian).
[4] 1381 *Rebellion of Jack Straw*, Wright, *Political Poems* (from Cambridge MS).

THE SAVOY

Henry VI the Savoy was again the object of attack according to Shakespeare:

(Cade) So, Sirs: now go some and pull down the Sauoy: others to th' Innes of Court, downe with them all.[1]

When the property devolved to the Crown, Henry VII commenced the rebuilding, with the intention of forming a hospital for 100 poor people. The King's intentions were set forth in his will, from which the following is an extract [2]:

to doo and execute vj out of the vij works of pitie and mercy by means of keping, susteyning and maynteynyng of commun hospitallis wherein if thei be duly kept, the said nede pouer people bee lodged, viseted in their sicknesses, refresshed with mete and drinke and if nede be with clothe and also buried, yf thei fourtune to die within the same

The scheme was fully completed in the next reign, and the Savoy ceased to be a Royal Palace. Nothing remains but the Chapel at the present time.[3]

In the reign of Queen Elizabeth the locality was in bad repute as the lurking-place of rogues and a retreat for debtors and those who had a reason for keeping out of the way. The Hall of the Hospital was a beautiful one and apparently was used for public purposes. At the Restoration it was the meeting-place of the Commissioners for the revision of the Liturgy. Isaak Walton alludes to this in his 'Life of Sanderson.' 'The place appointed for this debate was the Savoy in the Strand.' Dr. Sanderson, who was Bishop of Lincoln, presided, its object being to satisfy the conscience of those who ' could not comply with the services and ceremonies of the Church.'

The following is an allusion to some place in the locality, the exact position of which is not defined:

This is the Jesuit's house in the Savoy that secretly bears the name of their Founder [4]

---

[1] 1592. 2 *Henry VI* (1623, p 140)
[2] As quoted by Pennant.
[3] See *London Churches before the Great Fire*.
[4] 1660. Richd Carpenter, *The Pragmatical Jesuit, new-leven'd*, p. 32.

A LITERARY TOPOGRAPHY OF OLD LONDON

The Mastership of the Savoy seemed to be a coveted position. Cowley the poet was promised it by both Charles I and II, but failed to obtain it, hence the following line in a contemporary poem:

> Savoy-missing Cowley came into the Court.[1]

The house of the Duchy of Lancaster was in the vicinity, and the Chancellor of the Duchy lived there.[2]

The Savoy occupied one portion of the large area known as the Liberty of the Duchy of Lancaster, which extended west from the Temple as far as Ivy Bridge, and was bounded north and south by the Strand and the river. The name of Lancaster Place given to the modern street leading to Waterloo Bridge is a reminiscence. But according to Stow the House of Lancaster was not the first owner of the Liberty, which 'sometime belonged to Briane Lister, since to Peter of Savoy, and then to the House of Lancaster.'[3] And we hear of several Dukes there resident, and their establishment must have been on a large scale, as Stow devotes some pages to the details of an account seen by him of one year's housekeeping of Thomas, Earl of Lancaster (7 & 8 Edward II). This Thomas appears to have been the son of Edmund, Earl of Lancaster. Henry, the first duke of the title, was later.[4] The items of the account given by Stow[5] shew the most profuse and lavish expenditure, the total for one year being £7957 13s. 4½d. (considering the period, an enormous sum and indicating a palace of regal splendour). According to Shakespeare, 'old John of Gaunt, time-honour'd Lancaster,' was at Ely House when he died, and it was there that he had his final interview with Richard II.[6]

References to several minor palaces may occasionally be met with.

---

[1] a. 1665. *The Choice of a Laureate.*
[2] A model of the Palace as it appeared in 1650 has been executed by James P. Maginnis, A.M.I.C.E., and may be seen at the London Museum. The chapel may be seen, and a long range of buildings, Gothic in character, with low, square battlemented towers, some of which are no higher than the main buildings.
[3] *Survey of London* (1603), p. 445.
[4] *Dict. of Nat. Biog.*
[5] *Survey of London* (1603), p. 86
[6] *Richard II*, I. i. and II. i.

TOWER ROYAL

Scotland Yard at Charing Cross is a reminiscence of the old Palace of the Kings of Scotland. Stow, alluding to the place, says:

> Where great buildings have been for the receipt of the Kings of Scotland ... Margaret Queen of Scots had her abiding there when she came into England after the death of her husband.[1]

This may have been a previous visit and not the one already alluded to when her brother Henry VIII gave her Baynard's Castle.

Stow also speaks of an old palace in the time of Henry VI, situate in Old Jewry in the parish of St. Martin Pomary, and says the King 'gave the office of Porter to John Stent for the time of his life by the name of his principall Palace in the Old Jewrie.' He adds: 'In my youth called "The Old Wardrope."'[2]

A small street known as Tower Royal in Cannon Street marks the situation of an old palace of that name, said to date from the time of King Stephen; Stow says King Stephen was lodged there 'in the heart of the Citie, for his more safety.'[3]

The same historian says that in the reign of Edward I 'it was the tenement of Symon Beauwines,' and that in the reign of Edward III it was called 'the Royall' and in the next reign 'The Queen's Wardrobe.' He adds:

> King Richard (the second) having in Smithfield overcome and dispersed his rebels, hee, his Lordes and all his Company entered the Citty of London with great ioy and went to the Lady Princes his mother who was then lodged in the Tower Royall, called the Queene's Wardrobe.[4]

The place appeared to be well equipped for defence, as later events testified.

---

[1] Stow, *Survey* (1603), p. 455.   [2] *Ibid.* p. 284.   [3] *Ibid.* p. 248.
[4] *Ibid.* pp. 245-6. The name 'Royal' is by some considered to be derived from 'la Riole,' a place in Gascony from whence the Merchants of the Vintry imported wines. The name 'Royal' for 'Riole' is considered an error by many modern topographers, but the ancient house was certainly occupied by Royalty as a minor palace, and we hear of it being fortified and used as a place of refuge: therefore the term 'Tower' was not inappropriate. See Wheatley's *London* and Harben's *Dictionary* and Mr. Kingsford's note in his edition of Stow's *Survey*.

A LITERARY TOPOGRAPHY OF OLD LONDON

VII

Palaces remote from London do not fall within the scope of this work and can only be slightly alluded to; and indeed even those so important as Hampton Court and Windsor are but little referred to in 16th and 17th century literature.

Thomas May, in a poem 'The Victorious Reign of Edward III,' mentions Windsor :

> In Savoy Palace when the feast is ended
> King John of France is lodged and thence attended
> In fitting state to Windsor Castle.[1]

Henry VI was born here in 1421. Paul Hentzner, who visited it in Queen Elizabeth's reign, says it was supposed to have been begun by King Arthur and that the glorious King Edward III built it new from the ground. Gregory's 'Chronicle' (19 Edw III) has an allusion :

> And that yere the Kyng beganne the Rounde Tabylle at the Castle of Wyndesour that ys for to say the ordyr of the Knyghtys of the Gartyr

Hampton Court, built by Wolsey, and fortunately still with us and too well known to need description, was probably the finest specimen of Tudor domestic architecture of the time of Henry VIII. Harrison in his description of England (Holinshed's 'Chronicle,' *c.* 1577) extols King Henry VIII as 'the onlie phenix of his time for fine and curious masonrie' Speaking of the houses built in his own time, he says 'They are rather curious to the eie (like paper worke) than substantiall for continuance.' This wants qualification. He evidently believes in the solidity of massive brickwork; but even the timber-framed houses of Elizabethan times, and earlier (saving destruction by fire), lasted for centuries, and specimens are still standing.

We find occasional mention of the King's Palace at

[1] 1635 Lib 6

RICHMOND PALACE

Shene (the old name for Richmond), and Bacon tells us it was burnt down in the reign of Henry VII·

About this time a great fire in the night time suddenly began at the King's palace of Shene near unto the King's own lodgings whereby a great part of the building was consumed with much costly household stuff, which gave the King occasion of building from the ground that fine pile of Richmond, which is now standing.[1]

Shene (or Schenes) is the old name for Richmond in Surrey. Bacon uses both names, and his account reads as if the Palace built by Henry VII was not on the site of the old one which dated from the time of Henry I and is mentioned in an early Chronicle. 'The same yere was the Kynges grete werke begonne at Shene.'[2]

The Palace at Shene is frequently mentioned in the 'Paston Letters,' but when Henry VII writes 'To our trusty and welbeloved Knight, Sir John Paston' in 1500, the letter is.

Yeven under our signet at our Mannor of Richmount, the XX^{ty} day of Marche.

This letter was an important one, as it gave instructions to the trusty Knight to be in attendance on the expected arrival of ' the right excellent Princesse, the Lady Katherine . . . for the solempnization of matrimony betweene our deerest sonne the Prince [Arthur] and the said Princesse.'[3]

It was in the Palace of Richmond that the contract of marriage was signed, and within a very short period also the treaty for the intended second marriage with Henry[4]

The King formed a library there, and there are some notes as to the cost of books, but the information is somewhat vague, e.g., 'To a Frenshman for certain bokes £56 4s.' It was here that Henry VII died, as in later years did Queen Elizabeth. The small chamber over the gateway is said to have been occupied by her.

---

[1] Bacon, *Life of Henry VII* (1622), *Works*, 1862, p. 438. What remains of the old Palace of Richmond may still be seen near the Green.
[2] *A Chronicle of London*, 1089–1483.
[3] *Paston Letters*, vol. iii, Gairdner
[4] See T. R. Way and F. Chapman, *Ancient Royal Palaces*

A LITERARY TOPOGRAPHY OF OLD LONDON

Theobalds, near Cheshunt, was much favoured by James I, and he died there, as recorded by James Howell in one of his letters:

> It was my fortune to be on Sunday was fortnight at Theobalds where his late Majesty King James departed this life and went to his last rest on the day of rest, presently after sermon was done.[1]

Robert Carey writes in his 'Memoirs':

> The King fell sick of a tertian ague at Theobalds, and, to the grief of all true hearts, died of that sickness this 27th day of March [1625] in the twenty-second year of his reign.

Theobalds Park still exists, and the second Temple Bar, built by Christopher Wren, when removed from Fleet Street, was re-erected there, and may still be seen.

Nonsuch, near Ewell, a grand Tudor house often visited by Queen Elizabeth, has disappeared, though the Park still remains.

At Eltham in Kent the ruins of the banqueting hall of the old Palace still exist. 'Builded by King Henrie the third if not before.' So Harrison writes in his description of England contributed to Holinshed's 'Chronicle,' 1577, but it has been attributed to Edward IV. The earlier part was built by Anthony Bek, Bishop of Durham, who died in 1310. Edward III is said to have held a parliament there. Richard II used it, and Henry IV is said to have been married there by proxy.

The small Palace at Chelsea, favoured by Henry VIII, may be briefly mentioned. The King acquired the Manor from William Lord Sandys in 1536, and thus the Manor House became a Royal Palace. In the reign of Edward VI the Princess Elizabeth, with Queen Katherine Parr, lived there, and the ex-Queen Anne of Cleves died there. Chelsea had an attraction for Henry VIII at the period of his intimate friendship with Sir Thomas More, who lived there, but it could hardly have afforded pleasant memories after the latter's tragical end.[2]

---

[1] 1625 *Familiar Letters*, vol. ii iv. vii
[2] See article in *Gentleman's Magazine*, 1833, part ii p. 481.

VIII

GREENWICH PALACE

Greenwich is so close and accessible as to be considered part of London, and the Palace so frequently visited by Queen Elizabeth cannot be passed over without a more extended notice. Harrison, in his 'Description of Britaine,' referring to the Palace, says:

> Greenwich was first builded by Humphrey Duke of Gloucester upon the Thames side ... in the time of Henry the Sixth and called Pleasance, greatly enlarged by King Edward IV, garnished by King Henry VII, and finally made perfect by King Henry VIII the only Phenix of his time for fine and curious masonry.[1]

Named 'Placentia' by a later writer, who says:

> after magnificently enlarged by K Henry 7 and King Henry 8 and rendred famous for the birth there of severall great Princes, viz King Henry VIII, Queen Mary and Queen Elizabeth.[2]

Referring to the disgrace of the unfortunate founder, there is an early ballad entitled 'Fall of the great Duchess of Gloucester the wife of Duke Humphrey':

> Then flaunted I in Greenwich's stately towers
> My winter's mansion and my summer's bowers.[3]

The property fell to the Crown, and Stow tells us

> King Edward the 4 in the fifth of his reign gave to Elizabeth his wife the Mannor of Green witch with the Tower and Parke.[4]

We hear of Henry VIII there in the time of his first wife and how 'on May-day in the morning he rode a maying to the high ground of Shooters Hill.'[5] Another Kentish topographer tells us how lavish Henry was in his expenditure on the place:

> King Henrie the eight as he exceeded all his progenitors in setting up of sumptuous housing, so he spared no cost in garnishing

---

[1] 1577. In Holinshed's *Chron.*, B. II, c. 9.
[2] 1659. Kilburne's *Kent*, pp. 114–5.
[3] *The Crown Garland of Golden Roses*, part ii, 1659 (Percy Society).
[4] Stow, *Survey* (1603), p. 249.   [5] *Ibid.* p. 99.

A LITERARY TOPOGRAPHY OF OLD LONDON

Greenwiche till he had made it a pleasant, perfect and princely palace . . . his deer sonne King Edward (a miracle of Princely towardnesse) ended his life in the same house [1]

The Palace was specially a chosen resort at festive seasons. In 1512 Henry VIII kept Christmas there and presented what Sir Richard Baker calls 'one of his jovial devices.' This was a sham castle called '*la fortresse dangereuse*,' in which were '12 ladies cloathed in russet satten laid all over with leaves of gold.' The King and his company attack the castle, and of course the ladies submit. A mask was introduced 'after the manner of Italy, a thing not seen before in England.' [2]

King Edward VI kept his Christmas there in 1552, 'with open household.' Stow says, 'G Ferrers being lord of merry disports all the xij daies . . . the King had great delight in his pastimes.' [3] The George Ferrers alluded to was 'Master of the King's Pastimes' and 'Lord of Misrule' to Queen Mary. He is well known as the joint author of the 'Mirror for Magistrates.'

Queen Elizabeth, who was born there, made Greenwich her favourite home, more especially in the summer-time. Paul Hentzner, who wrote his travels in England in her reign, gives a graphic description of the magnificent state she there maintained :

We were admitted by an order procured from the Lord Chamberlain, into the presence-chamber hung with rich tapestry and the floor after the English fashion strewed with hay (? rushes) through which the Queen commonly passes in her way to Chapel. In the same Hall were the archbishop of Canterbury, the bishop of London, a great number of counsellors of state, officers of the Crown, etc.

Then came the procession to the Chapel with all the royal insignia :

Next came the queen, in the sixty-fifth year of her age, very majestic; her face oblong, fair but wrinkled ; her eyes small, yet black and pleasant,. her nose a little hooked ; her lips narrow

---

[1] W Lambard, *Perambulation of Kent* (1656), p. 474.
[2] *Chronicle*, 1643 (Ed. 1665, pp 273-4)
[3] *Summarie of Chronicles* (1598), p 269

GREENWICH PALACE

and her teeth black (a defect the English seem subject to, from their too great use of sugar) . . . she wore false hair and that red ; upon her head she had a small crown . . . her bosom was uncovered as all the English ladies have it, till they marry ; . . . her air was stately, her manner of speaking mild and obliging. That day she was dressed in white silk bordered with pearls of the size of beans and over a mantle of black silk shot with silver threads ; her train was very long, the end of it borne by a marchioness . . whoever speaks to her it is kneeling.

The Queen addressed all foreign Ambassadors in their own language, she, besides being well skilled in Greek and Latin, being mistress of French, Italian, Spanish, Scotch and Dutch. Hentzner was allowed to see the Queen's dinner table set out, which he describes as being done with punctilious ceremony amounting to solemnity. But, he observes, 'the Queen dines and sups alone with very few attendants.'[1]

Hentzner mentions the Park, stocked with deer. This was used by James I for hunting, and he had a wall built all round it.

Just after the Restoration Samuel Pepys visited Greenwich in company with Sir William Penn :

To Greenwich by water. Sir William and I walked into the Parke, where the King hath planted trees and made steps in the hill up to the Castle which is very magnificent. So up and down the house which is now repayring in the Queenes lodgings.[2]

Later on Pepys alludes several times to a new house that Charles II was building.

The Tower of London, a fortress originally, and in later times for the most part a state prison, was also at times a Royal Palace. Harrison in his 'Description of England,' touching on the traditional Kings of a remote period, says that 'King Belin held his aboad there' and extended the site that it stretched almost to the gate bearing his name (now Billingsgate).

[1] *Paul Hentzner's Travels.* Written in Latin, 1598, tr. by R. Bartley for Horace Walpole, Strawberry Hill, 1757 (1797, pp. 33-37).
[2] *Diary,* April 11, 1662.

A LITERARY TOPOGRAPHY OF OLD LONDON

But in another place the same writer says:

> The Tower of London is rather an armorie and house of munition and thereunto a place for the safe keeping of offendors than a palace roiall for a King or Queene to soiourne in [1]

But at all events down to the reign of Elizabeth and later it was occasionally used as a residence by our monarchs, and especially at the commencement of a reign, when the new and yet uncrowned King or Queen stayed there for a few days, and from thence made their progress to Westminster in great state for the coronation.

Another instance of royal occupation is recorded, but it was a matter of policy. Henry VII, at the time of the Perkin Warbeck rebellion, took up his residence at the Tower. The following is from Ford's play, based on Bacon's 'Life of Henry VII':

> It is our pleasure to remove our Court
> From Westminster to the Tower; we will lodge
> This very night there; give, Lord Chamberlain,
> A present order for it.[2]

Bacon gives the reason:

> Upon the morrow after Twelfth-day (1496) the King removed from Westminster, where he had kept his Christmas, to the Tower of London . . . And the place of the Tower was chosen to that end, that if Clifford should accuse any of the great ones, they might, without suspicion of noise or sending abroad of warrants, be presently attached, the Court and prison being within the cincture of one wall.[3]

To revert to earlier days, to the unfortunate Richard II the Tower was both Palace and prison. It was here he signed his abdication with—according to the old chronicler John Capgrave—complacency, if not with satisfaction and pleasure:

> Whan this tyme was come, evene on Mihelmesse day, the Kyng in the Toure with good-wil, as it semed and mery chere, red the Act of his Cessacion before the Lordis and other men present, etc. (1399).[4]

---

[1] 1577. Book ii. chap. xv.   [2] 1634. *Perkin Warbeck*, I, ii.
[3] Bacon, *Henry the Seventh*, 1622 (*Works*, 1862, p. 399).
[4] Capgrave's *Chronicle of England* (a. 1464), Rolls, p. 272.

KENSINGTON PALACE

One Royal residence must be briefly alluded to, although it lies beyond the confines of London and Westminster, and its use as a palace took place only at the end of the 17th century, and its history belongs chiefly to the 18th century, a period with which we are not now dealing

Heneage Finch, Lord Chancellor in 1674 and first Earl of Nottingham, owned and lived in the house at Kensington which bore his name, Nottingham House. His successor, the second Earl, sold it to William III for £20,000, and it became Kensington Palace. Originally a small house, it was enlarged by William III, and again added to by Queen Anne. The Palace still stands, and is known to every Londoner. 'It possesses a Dutch solidity,' was Leigh Hunt's comment.[1] Indeed it may be considered a good specimen of the Dutch style of brick-built domestic architecture, which prevailed in the time of William III and was further developed in the next reign, and has been repeated more or less down to our own time, the name of ' Queen Anne ' being generally mentioned to designate its features. Evelyn calls the Palace a villa, but that was before the additions by Queen Anne.

25 Feb 1689–90 I went to Kensington which King William had bought of Lord Nottingham, and altered but was yet a patched building, but with the garden, however, it is a very sweet villa, having to it the Park and a straight new way through this park.

There is a tradition that the early house was identical with that taken by Henry VIII as a nursery for the Royal children. If so, the Queens Mary and Elizabeth and their brother Edward spent some of their early years there.[2]

[1] See Leigh Hunt's *Old Court Suburb*. [2] *Ibid*

CHAPTER II

The Bishops' Palaces

THE London houses appertaining to the Bishoprics (Palace or Place were alternative terms, and sometimes 'Inne,' 'Hostelrie,' or 'Lodging') were situate in many cases by the river side on the north bank, though three were on the south side of the river, one in Thames Street, and others to the north of the Strand. In cases where they passed into the hands of lay owners, their names were generally, though not always, changed to those of their new proprietors.

Most of them were alienated from their original ecclesiastical use before Stuart times. A bishop could not with justice to his diocese, which might be hundreds of miles from London, reside at a distance for a long period of time, and the necessity for his presence in Parliament only occurred at intervals. Probably the rent obtainable for the Palace from some tenant of rank and high position, or the purchase money if sold, was of greater value to the See and to the Bishop personally, than the distinction of possessing a lordly mansion and the convenience afforded by its use. At the present day, out of twenty or more palaces existing in the sixteenth century, only two, viz. Lambeth and Fulham, are still with us.

I

Lambeth Palace, the residence of the Archbishop of Canterbury, is situate facing the river nearly opposite Westminster and was easily accessible by water, which, in early days, was the usual mode of approach, the journey

A LITERARY TOPOGRAPHY OF OLD LONDON

from Westminster to Lambeth by land over London Bridge being one of some three miles. The present Horseferry Road on the Middlesex side and Ferry Street on the Surrey mark the position of the old Ferry.

The Manor of Lambeth traditionally belonged to Hardiknut, and there it is said he died in 1042. In the 12th century the Manor was in possession of the Bishop of Rochester. In 1197 it became the property of the See of Canterbury by exchange, Glanville, the Bishop of Rochester, however reserving a small piece of land on which he afterwards built Rochester House. The Archbishop, Hubert Walter, intended to found there a new College,[1] but the scheme had to be abandoned and he decided to make use of the manor house as a residence. His successor, Stephen Langton, improved it. Boniface,[2] whom Pennant termed 'a wrathful and turbulent Primate,' rebuilt the place with great magnificence by way of expiation for his unruly and illegal conduct in connexion with the Prior of St. Bartholomew —so Pennant relates. Henry Chichele, or Chicheley, who was Primate from 1414 to 1443, is credited with having been the builder of what was sometimes called the Lollards' Tower at the west end of the chapel, the cost being recorded with great minuteness as amounting to £278 2s. 11¼d.[3] But this name was given to it after the Lollards' Tower at St. Paul's, one of the western towers of the Cathedral, was destroyed in the Great Fire. This prison at Lambeth, which may still be seen, was used for offenders, especially those against Church doctrine or discipline, and stories are told of cruel treatment. Pennant laments that so worthy a man as Chicheley should have built a prison-tower for Wickcliffites. Milton writes of it as 'Your Gehenna at Lambeth.'[4] It is said that the poet Lovelace was there confined and found his prison 'an hermitage' and was inspired with what has proved a stock quotation.

---

[1] Probably of secular canons. Pennant says 'Secular Monks,' but this must be an error. See Pennant's *London*, 1813 edit., p. 25.
[2] Boniface of Savoy, Archb. of Cant. 1244.
[3] See *Hist of Lambeth Palace* by Ducarel, 1785.
[4] *Animadversions*.

LAMBETH PALACE

The great tower and gateway are said to be the work of Archbishop Morton,[1] who died in 1500 and was a great builder in his time.

The Great Hall of the Palace was the work of Archbishop Chicheley and was pulled down by Thomas Scot, the regicide, who is said to have sold the materials for his own benefit.

The Palace, as the residence of the Primate, and therefore a symbol of Anglican episcopacy, was much hated by the Puritan party. The very word gives a contemporary poet an opportunity for moralisation.

> Lambeth was Oxford's Whetstone, yet above
> Preferments pinnacle they move
> Who string the universe and bracelet it for love [2]

In the Civil War, so soon as the Puritans had the predominancy in London

All the Bishops' houses were turned into prisons, and they filled with Divines that would not take the Covenant or forbear reading Common Prayer.

So Walton writes in his 'Life of Sanderson.' [3]

The same writer in his biography of Hooker (though he is treating of a period some fifty years earlier than the Civil War) hints personal motive in the Earl of Leicester's attempts to discredit the Bishops.

His design being to bring such odium on the Bishops as to procure an alienation of their lands ... his ambition and greedy hopes seemed to put him into possession of Lambeth House.

William Laud was Primate from 1633 till his execution in 1645, and by his arbitrary action in attempting to enforce conformity in Church doctrine and ceremony obnoxious to the Puritan views prevailing, had made bitter enemies of the majority of the laity. As Fuller puts it, he was accustomed ' to infuse more vinegar then oyle into all

---

[1] So stated by Ducarel in his *History of Lambeth*, but it is considered by some that portions of it were of earlier date.
[2] Edw. Benlowes, *Theophila*, 1652, C. I. lx
[3] 1678.

his censures.' The Palace was in danger of being wrecked by the mob. There is an entry in the Archbishop's diary :

> May 11, 1640. At midnight my house at Lambeth was beset with 500 of these rascal routers. I had notice and strengthened the house as well as I could, and God be thanked I had no harm. They continued there full two hours.[1]

Evelyn has a note to the same effect. He calls the mob ' a rude rabble from Southwark.'[2]

The storm at last burst over Laud's head, and he was impeached for high treason by the Long Parliament in 1640. His greatest enemy had always been William Prynne, who six years before had been sentenced by the Star Chamber to stand in the pillory in Palace Yard, to lose both his ears and to pay a fine of £5000. His chief offence was his book ' Histriomastix ' against stage plays, in which book he had cast reflections on the King (Charles I) and his Queen. His aggressive non-conformity was doubtless another offence, and on this ground Laud's influence was against him. Surely it was the acme of revenge for Prynne to be a witness of the Archbishop's arrest at Lambeth House. A friend of Prynne gives the incident :

> That pious and patient Saint and Sufferer . . . Master William Prynne, who coming to the Arch-Prelate's bedchamber betimes in the morning with a guard of soldiers to secure the business . . . sayes 'I am he whom you most unjustly and injuriously persecuted.'[3]

Another tract by the same writer gives an illustration (said to be the work of Hollar) shewing the entrance gate of the Palace with its two flanking towers, much as we see it now. The mob in front are about to make an attack. The plate is headed :

> The rising of prentises and sea-men on Southwark side to assault the Archbishop of Canterbury's house at Lambeth.[4]

---

[1] 1695, p. 58.   [2] *Diary*, June 1640.
[3] J. Vicars, *A looking-glasse for Malignants* (1643), A 4.
[4] John Vicars, *A Sight of ye Transactions of these latter yeares* (1646), p. 5. In the same book is a plate shewing the execution of Laud and others at Tower Hill. The executioner is holding up a head (B.M. E 365 [6]).

LAMBETH PALACE

The Chapel at Lambeth Palace has fortunately been preserved, but for many years the ancient crypt was so filled with dirt and rubbish that only the heads of the shafts and the vaulting were visible. The Archbishop in his account of his own trial writes :

> Dr. Featly said . . . that the Chappel lay nastily . . . was it one of my faults too to cleanse it ? Thirdly he says the windows were not made up with coloured glass till my time. The truth is they were all shameful to look on, all diversely patched like a poor Beggar's Coat. One Pember, a glasier, says there was in one of the glass windows on the north side the picture of an old man with a Glory which he thinks was God the Father. But his thinking so is no proof.[1]

The Puritans' hatred of painted windows must be borne in mind. In Archbishop Juxon's time the chapel was spoken of as being used for ' cellars and vaults.'[2] It would appear that the organ in the Chapel was the Archbishop's own property, as he bequeathed it in his will :

> I give to my successor (if the present trouble in the State leaves me any) my organ in the Chappel at Lambeth, provided that he leave it to the See for ever.[3]

Unfortunately it has disappeared.

The Great Gallery at the Palace was founded by Cardinal Pole and contained his portrait as well as those of some earlier Primates such as Warham (painted by Holbein) and Chicheley : also a portrait of Katherine Parr. There were two portraits of Archbishop Parker, one of them by Holbein In the dining room was Vandyke's portrait of Archbishop Laud and portraits of Archbishops Juxon and Tenison

Pennant says that the Library was founded by Archbishop Bancroft in 1610, the year of his death, but there may have been books there before a sufficiently ample room was built to contain them, for there is on record a letter from

---

[1] 1644. Archb. Laud's *Hist of his Trial* (1695), pp. 311–17. Presumably the Dr. Featly mentioned was Daniel Featly, at one time Rector of Lambeth and an opponent of Laud's innovations. He refused to turn the Communion Table ' altar-wise ' (See *Dict. of Nat Biog.*)
[2] See Ducarel's *Hist. of Lambeth*, 1785
[3] Will of Archb. Laud, 1643, proved 1661.

the Duke of Norfolk when imprisoned in the Tower in 1547 begging the loan of some :

> Most humbly to beseech my Lords that I might have some of the books that are at Lambeth · for unless I may have books to read ere I fall on sleep and after I awake again I cannot nor did not this dozen yeers.[1]

The Library was called 'The wonder of the world' in a rhyming tract of 1641, entitled 'Lambeth Faire's ended.' This was the year that the Palace was attacked by a mob :

> The wonder of the world, the great Library,
> Containing prayers as good as Ave Mary,
> Teaching how Priests and Deacons may be made,
> How they or any foole may worke o' the Trade ;
> But that which is most strange of all to tell—
> 'Twas said they had a holy Ghost to sell.[2]

In 1646, there being fear for the safety of the books, they were, on the suggestion of John Selden, sent to Cambridge University, but were returned after the Restoration and are still available to students. The Great Hall, already alluded to, was rebuilt and has since 1833 been used as the Library.

During the Civil War, Lambeth Palace, as already mentioned, did not escape the degradation of being turned into a prison, and for a time it was used for Royalist prisoners. Archbishop Laud writes in his 'History of the Troubles' (1642)

> It was resolved by the Honourable House of Commons to prepare an ordinance for the regulating of Lambeth House for a prison in the manner as Winchester House is regulated. And upon Jan. 5, 1642, a final order from both Houses came for the settling of Lambeth prison.[3]

Sir John Lenthall, son of Sir William Lenthall, the Speaker, was imprisoned shortly before the Restoration :

> I went to Sir John Lenthall at that tyme a prisoner in Lambeth House (for the Bishop's house was turned into a gaole and Leighton who was sentenced in the Star Chamber was the keeper).[4]

---

[1] Quoted in Lord Herbert of Cherbury's *Life of Henry VIII* (1649), p. 566.
[2] See Pennant's *London*   [3] *Op. cit.* (1695), p. 198.
[4] C. 1658, *Autobiog of Sir J. Bramston*, 1845, p 90.

LAMBETH PALACE

This was Alexander Leighton, a Puritan divine, who in 1628 had published a book entitled 'Sion's Plea against the Prelacie.'

The collection made by Archbishop Parker, a notable Primate of Queen Elizabeth's time, is of some interest. When he died an Inventory was made of his possessions at Lambeth House, and the whole were valued at £2766. The armour is described as:

> The Armour at Lambhith House viz. dymlaunes, corsletts, Brigandines, skulls, salletts, morians, calyvers, pikes, bowes, arrowes etc. prised at cj^{li} xiij nij^d.[1]

After the death of Archbishop Laud the See of Canterbury was vacant until the Restoration and there was no Archbishop at Lambeth. William Juxon was Primate for the brief remainder of his life (1660–1663) and was succeeded by Gilbert Sheldon, whose name survives in the Sheldonian Theatre at Oxford. It was in his time that Samuel Pepys paid his first visit to Lambeth and records, evidently with pleasure, a new experience of dining with an Archbishop, and the somewhat out-of-place entertainment given to a select number of the visitors in the afternoon. This consisted of the travesty of a Presbyterian sermon: a somewhat farcical kind of amusement, one would think, considering the place and the company. One wonders what William Prynne would have said.[2]

> March 14, 1669. At noon with M^r. Wren to Lambeth to dinner with the Archbishop, a noble house and well furnished with good pictures . . . exceeding great cheer, nowhere better. . . . I heard of a sermon that was to be there and so I staid to hear it, thinking it serious.
>
> But it turned out only a piece of mocking drollery by one Cornet Bolton . . . that behind a chair did pray and preach like a Presbyter Scot with all the possible imitation in grimaces and voice . . . exclaiming against Bishops etc.

---

[1] See *Archæologia*, vol. xxx. p. 30
[2] He died in 1669.

A LITERARY TOPOGRAPHY OF OLD LONDON

II

The Archiepiscopal Palace appertaining to the See of York and known as ' York House ' was originally designated ' Whitehall.' To quote Harrison, whose work was published with Holinshed's ' Chronicle ' :

' Whitehall was first a lodging of the Archbishops of Yorke.' The name is not uncommon and it would seem that the estate was so designated when owned by Hubert de Burgh, Earl of Kent, in the thirteenth century, by whom it was given to the Black Friars, who subsequently sold it to Walter Grey, Archbishop of York, who ' left it to his successors in that See for euer to be their house when they should repaire to the Cittie of London.'[1] Dugdale tells us there was a Chapel in Hubert de Burgh's time which was used by him.

> A free Chappel wherein to celebrate Divine Service for himself and his family . . . paying yearly to them [the monks of Westminster] a wax taper of three pounds weight upon the Feast-day of S Edward.[2]

An Archbishop of York is a character in Shakespeare's *Henry IV*, Part II, and one of the scenes is laid in a room of his palace. This was Richard le Scrope, who joined in the rebellion in favour of the Earl of March and was executed in 1405.

Before coming to the more important period of Henry VIII, we may mention incidentally that there was another York House in the time of Edward IV which demands brief notice. Lawrence Booth, Archbishop of York, 1476-80, and formerly Master of Pembroke College, Cambridge, and Dean of St. Paul's, bought land of a large area in Battersea, probably near some of the low-lying land in after years called Battersea Fields and in more recent times glorified into Battersea Park. Here he built a house which he occasionally occupied. In the time of the Civil War it was seized by the Parliament, but was eventually restored. The

---

[1] Stow's *Survey* (1603), p. 442.
[2] Dugdale's *Baronage* (1675), i. 699.

YORK HOUSE

present York Road is doubtless a reminiscence.[1] To return to the greater York Place, which attained the height of its fame in Wolsey's time and is always identified with the great Cardinal's name, Grafton in his 'Chronicle' says 'A fayre bishop's house,' though ' not fit for a King.'

Here the Cardinal lived in state and assumed the dignity and sometimes the judicial functions of a quasi-monarch. Thomas Deloney, in his life of Jack of Newbury, tells a story (and we note incidentally that he calls the place Whitehall):

> The Cardinall sent for the Clothiers afore him to Whitehall ... and there bestowing his blessing upon them, said ' Though you have offended mee I pardon you.'[2]

It seems there was a common report that the Cardinal was the son of a butcher, and that Jack of Newbury, a prosperous and well-known clothier whose name still survives at Newbury, had said:

> If my Lord Cardinalls father had beene no hastier in killing of Calues than hee is in dispatching of poor mens sutes, I doubt he had neuer won a Myter.

Wolsey's great wealth, combined with the knowledge and taste of a connoisseur, enabled him to turn York Place into a palace, somewhat—though not completely—on the scale of Hampton Court, which rivalled any King's Palace of the day. A story is told of Wolsey's arrogance, which may, or not, be true. The Pope, as customary, had sent him a hat:

> It came to Westmonstre where it was sette on a cupborde and tapers about so that the greatest duke in the londe must make curtesye therto, yee and to his emptye sete, he beinge awaye[3]

A satire of the time (c. 1528) has the following allusion:

> Grett palaces without compareson,
> Most glorious of outwarde sight
> And within decked poynt-device,
> More like unto a paradice
> Then an erthely habitacion.[4]

[1] See Cunningham and Wheatley's *London*.   [2] 1596, *op. cit* c vi
[3] *The Practyse of Prelates* (1530), W Tyndale, K v.
[4] W. Roy, *Rede me and be nott wrothe* (1871, p 57). Hampton Court and York Place are indicated.

A LITERARY TOPOGRAPHY OF OLD LONDON

Just before his fall, when the Cardinal was oppressed with gloomy forebodings, Sir Thomas More, who succeeded him in the Chancellorship, visited him:

> After the Parliament was ended, at his House in the Gallery at Whitehall, he [Wolsey] uttered unto him [Sir Thomas More] his griefes . . . and he [More] began to commend that Gallery and said, I like this Gallery of yours, my Lord, much better than your Gallery at Hampton Court.[1]

Cavendish, in his 'Life of Wolsey,'[2] alludes to a memorable entertainment at York Place:

> I have seen the King suddenly come in thither in a mask, with a dozen of other maskers, all in garments like shepherds, made of fine cloth of gold and fine crimson satin . . . and ye shall understand he came by water to the water-gate, without any noise.

This is the occasion when, according to Shakespeare, Henry first met Anne Boleyn. The scene was 'The Presence Chamber in York Place.'[3] Later on in the same play, the fall of Wolsey is related and the transfer of York Place to the King:

> You must no more call it Yorke-place, that's past;
> For, since the Cardinall fell, that title's lost:
> 'Tis now the King's, and call'd White-Hall.[4]

Whitehall, as enlarged, became a distinct Royal Palace, and eventually, but not by Henry, there was another York House provided for the Archbishopric. Lord Herbert of Cherbury tells us how:

> Our King (Henry VIII, 1532) having gotten Yorke-house (now White Hall) upon the Cardinall's conviction in a *Praemunire*, did newly enlarge and beautify it.[5]

The King's action was confirmed by Act of Parliament, a quotation from which may be cited:

> One great Mansion Place and House being parcel of the possessions of the Archbishoprick of York . . . and that he, the King, had upon the soil of the said Mansion Place . . . most sumptuously and curiously builded and edified many and distinct,

---

[1] W. Roper, *Life of Sir Thos. More* (1626), p. 28.
[2] 1562 (1885, p. 42).   [3] 1623, *Henry VIII*, I, iv.
[4] *Ibid.* IV, i.   [5] *Life of Henry VIII* (1649), p. 343.

YORK HOUSE

beautiful, costly and pleasant Lodgings etc. for his Graces singular pleasure, comfort and commodity . . . to be taken . . . and to be called the King's Palace and Westminster for ever.[1]

The King must have had a compliant Parliament, but it is difficult to see how the rights of the Church to Archiepiscopal property could be overridden.

George Cavendish, the biographer of Wolsey and a contemporary, was his Usher at the time of his fall and must have been present when the King's announcement of his pleasure was made to the Cardinal. Wolsey's reply was impressive. We quote from his book:

> In the mean time my Lord issued out of his Chamber and came to Master Shelley to know his message, who declared unto him, after due salutation, that the King's pleasure was to have his house at Westminster (then called York Place, belonging to the Bishopric of York) intending to make of that House a Palace Royal; and to possess the same according to the laws of his Grace's realm Master Shelley, quoth my Lord, . . . may I do it with justice and conscience, to give that thing away from me and my successors which is none of mine? . . . ye shall make report to the King's highness that I am his obedient subject . . . whose royal commandment I will in no wise disobey . . . Howbeit I pray you shew his Majesty from me that I most humbly desire his highness to call to his most gracious remembrance that there is both heaven and hell [2]

In Shakespeare's *Henry VIII*, Wolsey says to Cromwell:

> There, take an Inventory of all I have
> To the last peny, 'tis the King's [3]

A quotation from one of Wolsey's Inventories may not be without interest. The MS. may still be seen and read at the British Museum:

> Inventorie of Cardinall Woolseie Househould stuffe Temp. H. 8. The originall booke as it seemes kept by his own officers.

The above is in a later hand. The list follows. Only a few items are selected as specimens:

> The new hanginge of Counterfette Arras and Tapestry.

---

[1] Act 28 Henry VIII, as quoted by Strype
[2] Cavendish, *Life of Wolsey*, c. 1557 (1885, p 168). It may be inferred that the 'Master Shelley' mentioned was Sir William Shelley, Judge of the Common Pleas.
[3] Act III, sc. ii.

A LITERARY TOPOGRAPHY OF OLD LONDON

These are mostly scenes from Scripture history described. Articles of domestic use follow, e.g.:

> A fether bedde patched without a bolster length ij yardes, etc.
> Mattrass covered with ffyne hollande clothe for my lordes owne lying ... stuffed with carded wulle
> Cupboard clothes, Napkyns, Towells of diaper   Hangings of blew velvette, boordrid with clothe of golde etc.[1]

What was known as 'The Gallery' in Edward VI's time must have been something of a private apartment, for it was here that the young King when in bad health received Bishop Ridley on a very memorable occasion, he having just preached a sermon on the duty of charity:

> The same day after dinner the King sent for him privately into the Gallery at White-Hall, caused him to set in a Chaire by him, would not permit him to remain uncovered

and entreated his advice as to the best way he might discharge his duty. During the interview the King announced his intention of making over to the City the buildings and Church of the Grey Friars and Bartholomew's Hospital for the relief of the poor and sick, and for educational purposes; also the Palace of Bridewell for the reception of the

> poor by idleness or unthriftinesse as riotous spenders, vagabonds, loyterers etc. . . The King forthwith caused his letters to be written and would not suffer the Bishop to depart till hee had confirmed them with his hand and signet and enjoyned the Bishop to be the messenger,[2]

that is to the Lord Mayor.

The Archbishop of York being houseless, Queen Mary provided a new York Place in Southwark. This was Suffolk House, built by Charles Brandon, Duke of Suffolk: reverting to the Crown it was for a time a Mint, but, as Stow tells us:

> Queen Mary gave this house to Nicholas Heath (or Heth) Archbishop of York and to his successors for ever to be their Inne or

---

[1] Harleian MSS 604.
[2] Sir J Hayward, *Life and Raigne of King Edward the Sixt* (1630), pp. 407-410.

lodging for their repaire to London in recompense of York House neare to Westminster which King Henry her father had taken from Cardinal Wolsey and from the see of Yorke.[1]

But Archbishop Heath, wishing to be nearer to the Court (although he had a near neighbour in the Bishop of Winchester), sold this and in lieu thereof bought Norwich House (otherwise Suffolk Place) near Charing Cross which he left to his successors.[2] Stow describes it as 'next beyond Durham House . . . sometime belonging to the Bishop of Norwich and was his London lodging.'[3] It thus came about that there was a new York House at Charing Cross, which after the Archbishop ceased to use it had many occupants, from the time of Queen Elizabeth till the Restoration.

III

The Bishop of London's Palace stood in St. Paul's Churchyard on the Paternoster Row side and was burnt down in the Great Fire. It was known as 'London House,' and the existing 'London House Yard' marks the position approximately. Allusions to London House refer to it more as a place of reception or temporary residence of Royalty than as the habitual home of the Bishops, who perhaps preferred the quiet and retirement of their second residence at Fulham, which was but a short distance away. We hear of Henry VI being there, but more as a prisoner than a guest:

> And in dyner tyme Kynge Edwarde [IV] was late in and so went forthe to the Bisshoppes of Londone palece and ther toke Kynge Henry[4] and the Archebisschoppe of York and put them in warde the Thursday next before Ester-day.[5]

The young prince, rightly Edward V, was at a later date

---
[1] Stow, *Survey* (1603), p. 413.
[2] *Ibid.*
[3] *Ibid.* p. 454
[4] Henry VI, who died or was murdered in the Tower in 1471.
[5] Warkworth's *Chronicle*, c. 1471 (Camden Society), p. 15. See also Grafton's *Chronicle*, 'Edw. IV.'

practically a prisoner there under the 'protection' of his uncle. The old London Chronicle tells us:

> The iiij day of May (1483) he came thrugh the Cite . . . the Kyng Ridyng in blew veluet and the Duke of Glowcetor in black cloth like a mourner; and he was conveid to the Bysshoppys palass in London and there logid.[1]

In the old play, *True Tragedy of Richard III*, the boy's mother asks:

> But where is the Prince my sonne? (*Messenger*) He remains at London in the Bishops palace in the hands of the Protector.[2]

The removal of the young King to the Tower 'causyd no suspytion,' so Polydore Vergil writes:

> For that thusage ys at the Kings Coronation for the whole assembly to coom out from thence solemly and so procede to Westmynster[3]

'Two yeres after Henry VII, victor at Bosworth, was here lodged,'[4] and again in 1469 he received here

> An orator sent from the Pope which brought unto the Kyng a swerde and a cappe of mayntenaunce.[5]

Sometimes there was great state and hospitality on a large scale or, as Stow puts it, 'great householde hath beene kept, as appeareth by the great Hall.' Henry Machyn enters in his Diary, 1551:

> The ij day of November cam to London from Hamton Courtte and landyd at Bennard Castyll the old Qwyne of Schottes[6] and cam ryding to the Bishops Palles at Powlles with many lordes.

When the Pope issued his Bull against Queen Elizabeth, his emissaries posted copies of it on the Bishop's house. A contemporary writer says:

> The same bulles were plentiful but in secret sort brought into the Realm and at length arrogantly set upon ye Bishop of London's Pallace neere to the Cathedrall Church of Pauls.[7]

---

[1] *Chron. of London*, Vitellius, A xvi 1483.
[2] *Op. cit* (1594), Shaks. Soc., p 29
[3] *Op. cit* (1534), Camden Soc. xxix. 178.
[4] *Chron.* as in note 3.   [5] *Ibid.*
[6] Mary of Guise.
[7] *The Execution of Justice on England* (1583), D jv.

LONDON HOUSE

A tract of 1567 alludes to it as 'The monster Bull that roared at my Lord Byshop's gate.' And at a later date there were verses on the subject:

> Which Bull (fond Felton) thy unhappie hand
> Did fix upon that Prelates Palace gate
> Which doth by Paules high towring temple stand.[1]

Felton was arrested and hanged in 1570.

In the reign of Charles I, at the time when the removal of the Church of St. Gregory was mooted, the destruction of part of the Bishop's Palace was contemplated:

> My Lord Treasurer cannot save the hall and Chapel of London House; but down they must go to make a clear passage about Paul's Church.[2]

A University for London had been suggested by Sir George Bucke in the reign of James I. The subject seems to have been brought up again during the Civil War and an anonymous pamphleteer suggested that the Cathedral or the Bishop's house might be adapted for the purpose:

> Many great houses may be had and made Colledges of with so little alteration and Pauls Church and London House be the publike Schooles.[3]

After the Fire the Bishop of London occupied for a short period a large house in Aldersgate Street, formerly the residence of the Lords Petre and known as Petre House. At a still earlier time it was known as Dorchester House, the home of the Marquis of Dorchester.

IV

The Bishops of London were Lords of the Manor of Fulham from the time of the Conqueror, possibly earlier, for it is said to have been given to Erkenwald, who was

---

[1] *Mirror for Magistrates*; R. Nicolls, *England's Eliza* (1610), p. 792.
[2] Letter from Sir John North to Dudley North, March 22, 1637. See *Gentleman's Magazine*, 1846, part 11. p. 384.
[3] *Motives for the present founding of an University in the Metropolis* (1646), p. 3.

consecrated to the see in the year 675. At all events the connexion of the Bishops with Fulham appears in Domesday Book.

The name Fulham signified, so it is said, 'the home of birds '—according to Camden ' Volucrum Domus, the habitacle of birds.'

We hear of Bishop Ridley there in the time of King Edward VI.

> In the days of Edward the Sixth when Bonner was kept in prison, reverend Ridley having his bishopric in London, would never go to dinner at Fulham without the company of Bonner's Mother and Sister; the former always sitting in a chair at the upper end of the table.[1]

In the time of Queen Elizabeth, Edmund Grindal, Bishop of London, and afterwards Primate, writes ' From my country house at Fulham on the banks of the Thames.'[2]

In 1646 came the Act for the sale of Bishops' lands. Up to that date Bishop Juxon, who two years later attended King Charles on the scaffold, had been suffered to live in Fulham House in peace. It then passed into the hands of Richard Harvey, silk mercer, but the Bishop was reinstated after the Restoration,[3] and became Archbishop of Canterbury the same year.

Laud had more peaceful days at Fulham than in the stormy times when as Primate he took up his residence at Lambeth. He writes in his Diary ' Oct. 29, 1630, I removed my family from Fulham to London House.' While at Fulham he occupied rooms in the old Tudor quadrangle, which is the main approach to the house. The rooms are very small and appear to be much in the same condition as when the Bishop occupied them, the oak panelling being in a good state of preservation. This quadrangle was built by Bishop Fitzjames in the reign of Henry VII, and is somewhat similar in style to the earlier part of Hampton Court. The main buildings, the older part

---

[1] Thomas Fuller, *Good Thoughts in Worse Times*, 1647 (1830, p. 158).
[2] *Zurich Letters*, p. 108
[3] Sinclair's *Memorials of St. Paul's*, p. 198.

FULHAM PALACE

of which dates from the 16th century, contain the Hall, which, for a time used as a Chapel, was built by Bishop Fletcher in 1595; two libraries, one of which is known as 'The Porteus Library,' because it contains the books left by Bishop Porteus; the dining-room, in which are still treasured the portraits of all the bishops since the Reformation, the most valuable of which is that of Bishop Juxon by Vandyke.

The beauty of the gardens owes much to the care and outlay of Bishop Grindal. They were visited in 1687 by Ray the great botanist.

A water-colour sketch shewing the House as seen from the gardens, before the modern additions on that front were built by Bishop Howley, is preserved at the Palace. It shews a building in Tudor style with towers and battlements. No trace is left of the buildings of Norman times, but the ancient moat, said to date from pre-Norman times, still exists and encircles an area of some forty acres.[1]

The Deanery of St. Paul's stood (and as rebuilt still stands) on the south side of St. Paul's Churchyard, a few yards from Carter Lane. 'The Deanes lodging' (to quote Stow) 'is a fayre olde House.' The following extract alludes to it in connexion with Archbishop Laud:

'Laud, look to thyself, be assured thy life is sought as thou art the fountain of wickedness—Repent of thy monstrous sin before thou be taken out of the world. . . .' This libel was found in the Dean of Paules his house (1629).[2]

In the time of the Civil War the Dean was dispossessed and a Puritan divine, Cornelius Burges, occupied his house, and, so we gather from the author of 'Hudibras,' divided it into tenements:

He divided his Text . . . as Burges divides the Dean of Paul's house not into parts but tenements; that is so as will yield most money.[3]

[1] See Faulkner's *Hist. and Topography of Fulham*, 1813.
[2] Baker's *Chronicle* (1665), 'Charles I,' p 497. Also Laud's *Diary*.
[3] 1647. Sam. Butler and Sir John Birkenhead, *The Assembly Man*, 1716, *Post. Works*, i. 101.

A LITERARY TOPOGRAPHY OF OLD LONDON

At an earlier time Dean Nowell got into some trouble involving a law-suit. It appears that :

> Our house . . . joynyng closse to the Deane of Paules howse was freelie lette without takynge of any fyne by the Deane of Paules to a schollar in the Universitie of Cambridge beinge hys kynsman towards the mayntenance of hym at his studie, the rent beinge v^{li} iij^s iiij^d.[1]

V

The Bishop of Winchester's House was in Southwark, in what was called 'The Liberty of the Clink,' being a little to the west of the Church of St. Mary Overie. It is prominent in the foreground of most of the views of London taken from the south side—a building of some size and Gothic in character. Until the Civil War the Bishops lived there, but afterwards had a house at Chelsea.

Pennant says that the founder was unknown, but Stow has it that it dated originally from Norman times, being built by William Gifford, Bishop of Winchester about 1107, ' upon a plot of ground pertaining to the Prior of Bermondsey,' who, it seems, in 1366 sued the Bishop in the Court of Exchequer for £8 due for ' lodgings in Southwark.' [2]

The following quotation from John Bale seems to allude to some buildings which were an adjunct to the Bishop's house :

> I think a mã might finde as honest stuffe as this in the scooles of my Lord of Wynchesters rentes at banke-syde.[3]

The following alludes to rioting and looting at the time of Wyatt's Rebellion :

> Dyuers of the souldiers went to Winchester place where one of them beyng a gentleman began to shewe his game before all the cardes were full dealed   I meane to ryffle and spoyle which is indeede the determinate ende of theyr purpose.[4]

---

[1] 1590. *Egerton Papers* (1840), p 136.
[2] See Stow's *Survey* (1603), p. 409.
[3] *Actes of the English Votaries* (1550), pt i. p. 36.
[4] J. Procter, *Wyatt's Rebellion* (1555), Fol. 56.   According to Hearne ' This rare book . . . was always reckoned of great authority by such as are impartial.'

WINCHESTER HOUSE

If Wyatt's followers were mainly 'gentlemen' of this kind, one can understand the failure of his enterprize. According to Dr. Heylyn, who wrote many years after the event, the rebels had

> no purpose at all more than the sacking of Winchester House and the defacing of the Bishop's Library there.[1]

In the time of Queen Elizabeth the house gave a welcome to a Royal visitor:

> At London (1559) he [i e. the Duke of Finland, son of the King of Sweden] was received by diverse Knights and gentlemen of the Court and lodged at the Bishopp at Winchesteres place in Southwarke.[2]

In the reign of James I it would appear that the Bishop was in sympathy with the masques which were so much in vogue at the Court, and lent his house as a meeting place for the actors:

> The maskers with their attendants and diuers other gallant young gentlemen of both houses as their convoy, set forth from Winchester House which was the Rende vous towards the Court.[3]

The Puritan party regarded the Bishops' houses as 'voluptuous princely Palaces' and the Bishop was dispossessed for a time:

> Our unlucky lordly Prelates to live to see their voluptuous princely Palaces (as Winchester house and Ely house) turned into Prisons.[4]

John Selden speaks of a somewhat notable prisoner there:

> Sir Kenelm Digby was several times taken and let go again, at last imprisoned in Winchester House. I can compare him to nothing but a great Fish that we catch and let go again, but still he will come to the bait, at last therefore we put him into some great pond for store.[5]

---

[1] *Ecclesia Restaurata*, 1661 (1849, ii. 119).
[2] Sir John Hayward's *First four years of the Reign of Queen Elizabeth*, 1636 (1840, p. 37).
[3] *Masques of the Inner Temple and Grayes Inne . . . in the Banqueting house at Whitehall*, 1612.
[4] J. Vicars, *A looking-glasse or Malignants* (1643). A 3
[5] J. Selden's *Table Talk*, a. 1654 (Arber's Reprint, p. 56) The *Dict. of Nat. Biography* says Sir Kenelm Digby was banished in 1649.

A LITERARY TOPOGRAPHY OF OLD LONDON

John Aubrey says that it was here 'he practised Chemistry and wrote his book of Bodies and Soules.'[1]

Winchester House, or part of it, was still standing in the early part of the nineteenth century. A drawing was made by Gwilt which shews the dining-hall as a fine apartment having a circular window with geometric tracery.[2] The present Winchester Street and Winchester Wharf serve to remind us of the old Palace. The second Winchester House at Chelsea, already mentioned, was purchased in 1664 (by virtue of an Act of Parliament, 1663), it being at that time the residence of James, Duke of Hamilton. It was situate near the river at Cheyne Walk and remained the property of the see until 1822.

VI

The Bishop of Rochester (Gilbert Glanville) has already been alluded to as the original owner of the Manor of Lambeth, and as having reserved a small portion of land when he sold the estate to the See of Canterbury and as having built thereon a house for himself. Stow, writing four centuries later, says of ' Rochester Inne or lodging' that it was on the south side of Winchester House. This seems to indicate a position at some distance from Lambeth ; still, the site may have been part of the manor. The position is believed to have been a little to the east of Westminster Bridge. Stow adds that in his day it ' of long time hath not been frequented by any Bishoppe and lyeth ruinous for lack of reparations.'[3]

It is the Lambeth Rochester House that we find alluded to in the reign of Henry VII, the occasion being the arrangements made for the reception of the Princess Katherine of Arragon previous to her first marriage :

After her departure fro Croydon she shalbe conveied to my Lord of Rochestre his place beside Lambithe and ther loge that night and hir ladyes [4]

[1] *Short Lives*, I, 227.
[2] See articles in *Gentleman's Magazine*, May and June, 1815.
[3] *Survey of London* (1603), pp 409-10.
[4] *Letters and Papers Henry VII*, 1501, vol. i. p. 409.

ROCHESTER HOUSE

At her departure there was to be provided

> a palfray with a pylion richly arraied and led in hand [1]

Fisher, who was executed in 1535, was the last Bishop to live in the above Rochester House. According to Pennant the place fell into the hands of Henry VIII, who exchanged it with the Bishop of Carlisle for certain houses in the Strand. Rochester House thus became Carlisle House.[2] The Strand property, vacated by the Bishop of Carlisle, would appear to be the Carlisle House lying between the Savoy and Ivy Bridge, and which Stow says (1598) ' now belongeth to the Earl of Bedford '

At a later date the Bishop of Carlisle occupied the large house in Lincoln's Inn Fields at the corner of Queen Street. In 1649 this house was in the possession of the Earl of Leicester (or his daughter) though still called ' Carlisle House ' In the Earl's Journal he notes:

> My daughter Lisle was brought to bed of a boy and my son Lisle wrote to me at theyre house in Lincoln's Inn Fields called Carlile House.[3]

VII

The Place or Inn of the Bishop of Ely was on the north side of Holbourne, the present street, Ely Place, marking the position approximately. It had not the advantage of a river frontage as many of the Bishops' Houses, but it had the attraction of open country surroundings and its own grounds were 20 to 40 acres in extent. John de Kirkeby, Bishop, who died in 1290, gave the manor house for the benefit of his successor, William de Luda, who added to the property. Thomas Arundel, Bishop in 1374 (afterwards Archbishop of Canterbury), ' builded of new . . . his Manors in divers places, especially this in Oldbourne '

---

[1] *Letters and Papers Henry VII*, 1501, vol. 1, p. 409.
[2] It was evidently known as Carlisle House for many years. There is still a Carlisle Street in Lambeth which may be a reminiscence.
[3] *Sidney Papers* (1825), p 95

A LITERARY TOPOGRAPHY OF OLD LONDON

—so Stow tells us—and the old manor house became worthy of the name of Palace. Pennant says the Hall was seventy feet long, lighted by six Gothic windows. The entrance from Holborn was by a double archway There was an inner quadrangle, on one side of which was the Chapel. John of Gaunt died there in the reign of Richard II. Presumably the house had been lent or let to him by the Bishop when his own Palace of the Savoy was burnt by the insurgents. Shakespeare has a reference in his play of *Richard II* :

> *Bushy*—Old John of Gaunt is very sicke, my Lord,
> Sodainly taken and hath sent post haste
> To entreat your Majesty to visit him.
> *Richard*—Where lies he ?
> *Bushy*—At Ely House [1]

The Black Prince was at one time lodged at Ely House, and from thence issued an order that a Tun of Wine should be sent to his old nurse at Oxford.[2]

The garden at Ely House was a special feature and was famous for its strawberries—so we may gather from Shakespeare's *Richard III* :

> My Lord of Ely [so the King says]
> When I was last in Holborne
> I saw good strawberries in your garden there
> I doe beseech you send for some of them [3]

The house being spacious and suitable for entertaining on a large scale, it was often lent, as was the custom, for some important banquet at which the Bishop was not the host. The Serjeants-at-law were on several occasions most magnificently hospitable, but in 1464 made a mistake in etiquette which spoilt the feast. The Lord Mayor and Sheriffs being invited on the same occasion as the Lord Treasurer, the latter was given precedence at table, which so offended the City magnates that they left the place.[4] In

---
[1] 1597. *Richard II* (1623, I, iv).
[2] Mentioned in his Diary, the MS of which is at the Public Record Office.
[3] 1597. *Richard III* (1623, III. iv.).
[4] Stow's *Survey* (1603), p 389

ELY HOUSE

the reign of Henry VIII, 1531, eleven of the Serjeants outdid all former efforts at profuse display. They kept feast for five successive days, on the first of which the King with Queen Katherine of Arragon were guests and among others there were present the Lord Mayor, the foreign Ambassadors, the Judges, the Master of the Rolls, and many others. Stow gives details as to the provisions provided and the cost, which are of some interest as indicative of the prices of food at the time, e.g. (quoting Stow):

> There were brought to the slaughter house 24 great Beefes at 26 shillings 8 pence the peece; one carkasse of an Oxe at 24s; one hundred fat muttons ijs xd the peece . . . Capons of Kent 9 dozen and sixe at 12d the peece . . . Pullets the best 2d ob. etc.

Like many other Bishops' Palaces, Ely Place appeared to be let at times. For example, in the reign of Edward VI we read in Sir John Hayward's Life of the young King:

> The Lords at London . . . sent for the Maior and Aldermen of the City to the Earle of Warwickes lodging at Ely House in Holborne. Here they presented themselves secretly armed.[1]

At a much later period we find the Earl of Southampton dating his letters from Ely House.

A large portion of the garden and orchard of the Palace was alienated from the See by the arbitrary action of Queen Elizabeth, to afford a site for the house that Sir Christopher Hatton designed to build. Naturally the Bishop of the time, Richard Cox, raised objections and received a personal letter from the Queen in which Elizabeth does not appear at her best. The action was illegal and the letter, as Pennant describes it, ' as insolent as indecent.' Being short it may be cited, although well known:

> Proud Prelate! You know what you were before I made you what you are now; if you do not immediately comply with my request, by God I will unfrock you.—Elizabeth.

It may be noted that although he had spent four years in exile, the previous career of Bishop Cox was a distinguished one. He was a Fellow of King's College, Cambridge; Head

---
[1] *Op. cit* 1630 (1636, p. 207).

A LITERARY TOPOGRAPHY OF OLD LONDON

Master of Eton ; Vice-Chancellor of Oxford and Bishop of Norwich.[1]

In the reign of James I., Count Gondomar, the Spanish Ambassador, a man much disliked, seemed to be residing at Ely House, Sir Christopher Hatton's new house having been built for some years, and the builder and the Bishop he had wronged both having passed away. James Howell tells us in one of his ' Familiar Letters '

> He [Count Gondomar] could do no good upon the Lady Hatton whom he desir'd lately, that regard he was her next neighbour, he might have the benefit of her back gate to go abroad into the fields ; but she put him off with a compliment [2]

At about the same time the Water Poet has an allusion to Gondomar (or to his successor from Madrid) who was one of those to welcome Prince Charles on his return from Spain where his wooing of the Spanish Princess had come to a somewhat undignified termination.

> Among the rest the Spanish Ambassadors both at the Exeter House in the Strand and at Ely House Holborne did express their loves by their charges and rejoycings [3]

During the Civil War the House was used for the accommodation of the sick and wounded

In the ' Rump Songs ' which appeared in the early days of that period Ely House is alluded to :

> I cannot say, I say, that I am one
> Of th' Church of Ely House or Abington
> Nor of those precious spirits that can deal
> The Pomegranates of grace at every meal.[4]

The allusion is to the Chapel or the services there.

This beautiful 14th-century church with its undercroft, surpassing any of those attached to the other Bishops' Palaces, has fortunately been preserved, and is still with us

---

[1] *Dict of Nat Biog.*
[2] *Op cit* (1622), Bk I. sect III no. 3. It is said that Gondomar, who was satirized in Middleton's play of *A Game of Chess*, when he returned to Spain, took with him a copy of the Folio of Shakespeare's plays published in 1623.
[3] J. Taylor (1623), *Prince Charles' Welcome Home*
[4] C. 1642, *Rump Songs* (1662, p 200)

ELY HOUSE

as the Church of St. Etheldreda.[1] It is in good preservation and has been for some time in the hands of the Roman Catholics.

The Palace has long since passed away. In the 18th century being in disrepair an Act was passed to enable the Bishop to alienate the property, provision being made to build a new Ely House in Dover Street.[2]

A small Inn called 'The Mitre' may still be seen in a Court leading out of Ely Place. It bears the sign of a Bishop's Mitre and is a reminder of glory departed

VIII

Near to Ely Place, but on the other side of Holborn, was the Bishop of Lincoln's House. It was near or probably on the site of the old Temple or part of it. According to Stow it was built about 1147 by Robert de Curars (or Querceto), Bishop of Lincoln, and 'John Russell, Bishop of Lincolne, Chauncellor of England in the raigne of Richard the third, was lodged there.'[3]

There is some discrepancy about this date, for the new Temple was not finished till about 1185. There is reference in the Patent Rolls to the fact of King John visiting Hugh, Bishop of Lincoln, in the year 1200 at ' the old Temple where he lay sick of the fever.'[4] This was Saint Hugh of Avalon who died in 1200. If this story be true it would indicate that the old Temple or part of the buildings had become the Bishop's residence. Stow says that the 'Old Temple was left and fell into ruine since the year 1184.'[5] But we hear of a bishop still there in the reign of Edward II.[6] More-

---

[1] See *London Churches before the Great Fire*, p. 248.
[2] This was on the site of Albemarle House, which was purchased out of the proceeds of the sale of the Holborn Estate
[3] Stow's *Survey* (1603), p 441
[4] See *Description of the Patent Rolls in the Tower of London* by Thomas Duffus Hardy (1835), p. 170.
[5] *Survey* (1603), p 441
[6] *Calendar of Close Rolls*, 17 Edward II, March 27 and June 10, 1324.

over there was a Letter Patent of John Bishop of Lincoln dated 'the old Temple, 1 Mar. 1379.'[1]

Of the Bishop of Chichester's Palace in Chancery Lane Stow writes:

> The King [Henry III] granted to Raph, Bishop of Chichester, Chancellor, the place with garden that John Herlison forfeited in that street called New Street [Chancery Lane].[2]

'Chichester Rents' and Bishop's Court, also Neville Court on the east side of the street, still remain in evidence. Of this (Chichester Place) Matthew Paris writes in his 'Chronicle':

> Ralph de nova villa or Neville, Bishop of Chichester and Chancellor of England, sometime builded a noble house even from the grounde, not far from the New Temple and House of Conuertes, in the which place hee deceased in the yeare 1244. [So quoted by Stow.]

It was in this year 1244 that we gather the property fell into the hands of the Crown. There is a Mandate in the Close Roll, 28 Henry III:

> De domibus Cycestrensis episcopi capiendis in manum regis et aliis.[3]

According to Stow, the Bishop of St. David's had a house near the Black Friars:

> The Bishop of S. Davids had his Inne over against the north side of this Bridwell.[4]

Nearly all the Bishops' Palaces were situated to the west of St. Paul's and in many cases in the district of the Strand. The Bishop of Hereford's Place was one of the exceptions, being the ancient home of the Mounthaunt family, standing on the west side of Old Fishstreet Hill. Radulphus de Maydenstone, Bishop of Hereford about 1234,[5] bought it from the Mounthaunts and gave it to the See of Hereford. The small Church of St. Mary Mounthaw was a Chapel attached to the House which Charles Booth,

---
[1] *Calendar of Patent Rolls*, 3 Richard II
[2] *Survey* (1603), pp. 441, 442.
[3] *Calendar of Close Rolls*, 28 Henry III, p. 154.
[4] *Survey* (1603), pp. 398.
[5] He resigned in 1239 in order to enter the Franciscan Order. See *Dict. of Nat. Biog.*

SALISBURY HOUSE

Bishop, repaired in 1517, but it afterwards fell into decay and was converted into small tenements. When Stow wrote his 'Survey of London' in 1598 he said, 'The Hall and principal rooms are an house to make sugar loaves.'[1]

A Welsh Bishop had a residence in Shoe Lane, Holborn, adjoining the Churchyard of St. Andrew's Church. This was Bangor House, mentioned as early as 1349; it was leased in 1540 and sold in 1647, but at the Restoration it reverted to the Bishopric. David Dolben was the last Bishop who is said to have resided there (1631). The name of Bangor House is still retained to designate the modern building on this site, viz. 66 Shoe Lane.[2]

Near the Strand Bridge was the House of the Bishop of Llandaff. This must have been built before the year 1311, for Stow notes that in the fourth year of Edward II the Bishop purchased a piece of land near the Church of St. Mary-le-Strand to enlarge his house.

IX

From Blackfriars westward we can trace the Bishops' Houses between Bridewell and Charing Cross.

The ancient 'King's House' which stood near St. Bride's Church being disused fell into ruin and decay. A portion of the site was used by Henry VIII for the erection of his new Bridewell Palace, but the western portion at an earlier date became the property of the Bishop of Salisbury, who there built his Palace, sometimes called Salisbury Court. The position is marked by the present Salisbury Square, Fleet Street.

In Gregory's 'Chronicle,' 18 Richard II, there is an allusion to a certain William, Bishop of Salisbury, who was 'Treasurer,' and we are told that:

> The servandys of the sayd Tresyrer raysyd grete debate and dycensyon in the Citte of London that was in Flette Strete for an hors i-lost where fore the Tresurer complaynyd unto the Kyng uppon the citte.

[1] Edit 1603, p. 357.
[2] See Harben's *Dictionary of London*. Not mentioned by Stow.

A LITERARY TOPOGRAPHY OF OLD LONDON

The result was that 'the Kyng dyd sesyn franches and ye lybertys of London fro them and removyd the Courte unto Yorke.' Serious punishment it would appear for the loss of a horse.¹

It was here in 1502, the same year that his brother died, that Henry, then 11 years old, entered into contract of marriage with Katherine of Arragon, his deceased brother's widow. As Sir Richard Baker writes in his 'Chronicle':

> On the five and twentieth day of June in the Bishop of Salisburyes house in Fleet Street the marriage was solemnized.²

Baker means contract of marriage. He himself records the actual marriage in the first year of Henry's reign:

> On the third day of June (1509) he [Henry VIII] married the said Lady at the Bishop of Salisburies house . . . to show she was a virgin widdow she was attired all in white and had the haire of her head all hanging downe behinde at the full length.³

Another early incident is related in Fabyan's 'Chronicle':

> A baker's man beryng a basket full of horse brede. . . . When he came for agayne the bysshop of Salesburyes place standyng in Salisbury Aley a seruant of the bisshoppis start unto the basket and toke out one of the louys.⁴

Hence there was a riot and bloodshed.

X

The first house west of the Temple and situate between the Strand and the river was the Palace of the Bishops of Exeter. Pennant has it that it was founded by Walter Stapleton, Bishop and Treasurer of England in the reign of Edward II; but Stow says he has not heard who the first builder was, but that Walter Stapleton was a great builder. He came to an untimely and unhonoured end

---

¹ Gregory's *Chronicle* (1395), Camden Society, p. 94.
² 1643. Baker's *Chronicle*, ' Henry VII,' p. 153.
³ *Ibid.* ' Henry VIII,' p 1.
⁴ *Op. cit.*, 1516, ' Richard II,' fol. 151.

EXETER PALACE

which Stow alludes to with brevity and a curious lack of explanation:

> The citizens of London when they had beheaded him in Cheape neare unto the Cathedrall Church of S. Paule, they buried him in a heap of sand or rubbish in his own house without Temple Bar where he had made a great building.[1]

Pennant's comment is that the victim to mob-law was ' unfortunately a favourite with Edward II in those factious days ' and therefore (here we quote Baker's ' Chronicle '[2]) ' the Londoners to shew their love to the Queen seized upon Walter Stapleton, the good Bishop of Exeter, left Governor there by the King, and with great despight beheaded him.'[3] Stow adds that Edmund Lacie builded the great hall in the reign of Henry VI and was Bishop when he died in 1455. John Arundel, Bishop in 1502, died at Exeter Place in 1503 and was buried at the Church of St. Clement Danes ' beneath a tomb with his figure expressed in brass.'[4]

The ancient Palace of the Bishops of Bath stood facing the river to the west of Essex House.

When Cardinal Campeggio visited England on the important occasion of the proposed divorce, he resided at Bath Place, and Wolsey in a letter alluded to it as if it were his, Wolsey's, property:

> He [Cardinall Campeggio] was escorted to Bath House belonging to the writer, who had given orders for it to be prepared and decorated with elegant furniture and everything necessary ... had the Pope come in person he could scarcely have been welcomed with more magnificent pomp.[5]

Cardinal Campeggio himself records his visit:

> In the morning the Cardinal [i.e. Wolsey] conveyed me to the river and I proceeded in a barge to the lodging assigned to me, namely Bath House, without noise or pomp.[6]

---

[1] *Survey of London* (1603), pp. 445-6.   [2] 1643, p. 151.
[3] He it was who founded Stapeldon Hall, afterwards Exeter College, Oxford.
[4] Pennant's *History of London*.
[5] Card. Wolsey to Bishop of Worcester, Ambassador at Rome *Venetian State Papers*, 11. 1355
[6] 1528. Card. Campeggio to Salviati, *Letters and Papers*, Henry VIII, 4857.

A LITERARY TOPOGRAPHY OF OLD LONDON

Cavendish in his 'Life of Wolsey' gives the incident and adds that the two Cardinals (who were joined in a commission to try the question of Queen Katherine's marriage to Henry VIII) ' went together to Bridewell directly to the Queen's lodging.'[1] This does not tally with an earlier passage of Cavendish[2] that ' the Legate Campeggio came by water in a wherry to *his own house* called Bath Place.'

In the same reign the house received royal visitors as related in the *London Chronicle*:

> Then came yn the Kyng of Denmark and his quene and lay in ye Bisshop of Bathes place wt oute Tempull bar.[3]

In after years the Bishop's Place enjoyed great fame as ' Arundel House.'

Near by, in the Strand, were two Bishops' houses, both of which were destroyed by the Protector for the sake of the material when Somerset House was in course of building.

> Many well disposed mindes conceived a hard opinion of him for that . . . two Bishops houses were pulled downe to make a seat for his new building

So writes Sir John Hayward in his 'Life of Edward VI.'[4] The one was the Inn of the Bishop of Chester and Coventry,[5] built by Bishop Walter Langton in the reign of Edward I (afterwards an Inn of Chancery).[6]

The other, which adjoined, was the Bishop of Worcester's Inn. Opposite, in the Strand, was a stone cross of some fame. Stow writes that:

> In the yeare 1294 and diuers other times the Iustices Itenerantes sate without London at the Stone Crosse over against the Bishop of Couentries house and sometimes sate in the Bishops house.[7]

---

[1] 1885, p. 125.
[2] *Ibid.* p. 112.
[3] *Camden Miscellany*, iv. 8.
[4] 1636, p. 204
[5] Stow says ' commonly called of Lichfield and Coventrie,' *Survey* (1603), p. 446. See also Brayley's *Londiniana*, 1829, iii. 134–5.
[6] In Thornbury's *London*, iv. 17, a later Chester House in Tothill Fields is mentioned with the date 1488.
[7] *Survey* (1603), p. 447.

XI

DURHAM PALACE

John Norden, writing of the Episcopal Palace of Durham in 1592, says:

> The howse called Durham or Dunelme howse ... apperteyned to the Bishopes of that Sea [sic]. ... It was a howse of 300 years antiquitie; the hall whereof is stately and high supported with loftie marble pillers. Her Matie hath committed the use thereof to Sir Walter Raleigh.[1]

The original Palace was built by Anthony de Beck, Patriarch of Jerusalem and Bishop of Durham in the reign of Edward I. Richard de Bury, Bishop of Durham, who died in 1345, lived here, and is well known as the author of 'Philobiblon.' He was a great collector of books and founded Durham College, which he enriched with a library, and made a similar gift to Oxford for Durham College there, which was dissolved by Henry VIII, and at a later date re-founded as Trinity College. Cuthbert Tunstall, Bishop of London and afterwards of Durham in 1530, was deprived by Henry VIII, who took the house into his own hands, but the Bishop was allowed the use of 'Cold Harbour' for a time. He was restored by Queen Mary but, refusing the oath of Supremacy, was again deprived by Queen Elizabeth. Harrison in his 'Description of England,' written in Queen Elizabeth's reign, says:

> East of this [i.e. of Whitehall] standeth 'Durham Place sometime belonging to the Bishops of Durham but converted by Henry VIII to a Palace roiall and lodging for the Prince.[2]

Durham Place had an important after-history which does not fall within the scope of this article. The small thoroughfare near Charing Cross called Durham-house Street is a reminder of the position of the old Palace.

---

[1] Norden's *Middlesex*, Harl MSS. 570 (Camden Society, 1840).
[2] *Op. cit.* (1577), Furnivall's edition, i. 268.

CHAPTER III

The Houses of the Nobles, Statesmen, and Citizens of Distinction

CHAPTER III

The Houses of the Nobles, Statesmen, and Citizens of Distinction

I

IN the many views of London as seen from the river, Baynard Castle, situate at the west end of Thames Street, is perhaps, after the Tower of London itself, the most strikingly prominent. Its long frontage on the river with its massive towers and bastions washed by every tide distinguished it from any of the Palaces and great houses westward of Blackfriars, though it had not as they had the setting of extensive grounds with river wall and water-gate. Originally a fortified place, it, at times, ranked among Royal Palaces, as many of our Kings lived there for short periods, and we find it continually used by Royalty on occasions of the highest importance. The building dated from the time of the Conqueror and took its name of Baynard from one of William's Norman followers. It was forfeited to the Crown in 1111.[1] According to the 'London Chronicle' the place was destroyed in the reign of King John, as we read in the Chronicle '

In this yere (13 King John) was Castle Baynard done and destroyed.[2]

But it was rebuilt, as it was in this reign, according to old tradition, that the Lord Robert Fitzwalter held it whose

[1] Pennant.
[2] *London Chronicle*, *Harl MS*, edit. by Nicolas, 1827.

daughter Matilda fled to Dunmow Abbey to escape the pursuit of the King, and was there poisoned by the order of John. Such is the legend preserved by Michael Drayton.

> Thus Baynard's Castle boasts my blessed birth
> And Dunmow kindly wraps me in the earth [1]

In the year 1275 the Castle was granted to the Archbishop of Canterbury, licence being given to Robert, son of Walter, to demise it ' saving the right of the King and others therein.' [2]

In 1428 the Castle was burnt. It seems to have changed hands, for we hear of its rebuilding by Humphrey Duke of Gloucester, and by his death it came into the hands of Henry VI and afterwards to the Duke of York. This new Baynard's was not on the site of the old one but a little more to the east.[3] Edward IV here assumed the name and dignity of King in the lifetime of Henry VI. It would appear, according to a play of Thomas Heywood, that Edward's unfortunate brother the Duke of Clarence lived here:

> *D. of Clarence* to *D. of Gloster*—
> Then brother I beseech you
> Plead you mine innocence unto the King
> And in meantime to tell my loyalty
> I'll keep within my house at Baynard's Castle
> Until I hear how my dread sovereign takes it.[4]

Richard III, if he did not live there, used it before his Coronation.

> Meet me within this houre at Baynards Castle

we find in Shakespeare's play. It was there that the

---

[1] *Matilda the Chaste* (1596), 156.

[2] *Calendar of Patent Rolls*, Edw I, p 96. In the *Calendar of Charter Rolls* of Edward I we find (Jan. 6, 1278) that ' the archbishop of Canterbury (Robt. de Kilwardby) restored to the King the site of Castle Baynard, which he had purchased' At a later date it would appear that the ' Friars Preachers ' were there. See *Calendar of Charter Rolls*, vol. v. 309

[3] So Mr. Kingsford says in a note in his edition of Stow's *Survey*, vol. ii pp 279-80.

[4] 1600. 2 *Edward IV*, II. iii. (Shaks. Soc).

BAYNARD'S CASTLE

Crown was offered to Richard by the citizens, and at first declined with feigned humility, as we may read in the older play:

> Whereupon in the afternoone came downe my Lord Mayor and the Aldermen to Baynard's Castle and offered my Lord to make him King, which he refused, so faintly that if it had been offered once more I know he would have taken it.[1]

A later historian has this comment on the incident:

> The next we hear is of a petition to the Protector at Baynard's Castle to take upon him the rule and government of the Realm as rightful King to which with much ado and entreaty (poor man!) he at last yielded—So slips this dissembling Yorkist into the throne over his young Nephew's head.[2]

Henry VII restored (some accounts say rebuilt) Baynard Castle. A MS in the Cotton Library speaks of it as

> seitt upon the Thames side, right pleasantlie towards the water, within well furnished and arraied full stronglie with walles encompassed withoute, etc.[3]

Here he (Henry VII) met and entertained the young Princess Katherine of Arragon, aged eighteen, on her arrival in England for her marriage with Prince Arthur, then aged fifteen. A contemporary account (1501) has been printed:

> And when the King in his said barge shall sette forth from the said Baynardes Castell then alle thoder barges and bootes to rowe by the King and about the King . . . till the tyme his grace shalbe landed at the great bruge of Westminster.[4]

The Castle was sometimes placed at the disposal of royal visitors. Henry VIII gave the use of it to his sister Margaret (late Queen of James IV of Scotland) and her second husband the Earl of Angus at a time when there

---

[1] 1594 Anon. play, *True Tragedy of Richard III* (1844, p. 32). This incident is the subject of a fresco painted by Sigismund Goetze, and placed in the present Royal Exchange.
[2] W Gough, 1682, *Londinium Triumphans*, p 325
[3] *Somers' Tracts*, I. 31.
[4] 'Reception of Katherine of Arragon' (1501), *Letters, etc., Hen. VII*, 1. 405.

were troubles in Scotland, but, as the old chronicle relates, the ' Earl of Angwyshe '

> lyke unto the nature of his Cuntre, went howme agen to Schotlande, takyng no love; wherefore the Kynge sende for her to London wher sche was rially receyved and logged at Baynards Castell (1516).[1]

When Edward VI died and there was a rival claimant to the throne in the person of Lady Jane Grey, the city stood by Queen Mary

> In Baynard Castle was a Council held
> Whither the Mayor and Sheriffs did attend
> And 'twas concluded to proclaim Queen Mary.[2]

At this time the Castle seems to have been in the possession of William Herbert, Earl of Pembroke, whom in after years Queen Elizabeth honoured with a visit, going on the water after supper. The following from the 'Sydney Papers' shews the Pembroke family still in possession at the end of Queen Elizabeth's reign:

> My Lady Pembroke hath againe sent Order . . . to make ready Baynard Castell for your Lordship and my Lady. . . . In your next unto her, I pray you take knowledge of this great Fauor she doth you [3]

The Castle was garrisoned by troops in 1648. It was burnt down in the Great Fire. There is a good view of the place as it appeared about 1640. We see a centre tower and two corner ones: seven bays in the space between. There is no trace of Norman work, the windows being Tudor in character. There is an entrance from the river with a very wide flight of steps.[4]

After the Restoration we hear of Royalty again at Baynard's. Samuel Pepys informs us:

> My Lord went at night with the King to Baynard's Castle to supper.[5]

[1] *Chron. of London*, iii Vitellius A, xvi
[2] Dekker and Webster, *Famous History of Sir Thos. Wyatt* (1607), III ii
[3] 1597 Rowland Whyte to Sir Robt Sydney, *Sydney Papers*, vol ii. p. 81
[4] See *London before the Great Fire*, G. F. Boydell, 1818.
[5] *Diary*, June 19, 1660.

YORK HOUSE, CHARING CROSS

Next to Baynard's Castle was Somerset Inn. Eleanor, Duchess of Somerset, daughter of Richard Beauchamp, Earl of Warwick, was living there in the reign of Edward IV.[1]

II

The original York House occupied by Cardinal Wolsey and afterwards the King's Palace of Whitehall, also the second York House afterwards appropriated to the use of the Archbishop of York, have been alluded to in the Chapter on the Bishops' Houses. References to the after history of this second York House are of some interest. Sir Nicholas Bacon, Lord Keeper, was in occupation in the early days of Queen Elizabeth, and his more famous son Francis was born there in 1561 and lived there for some years. Another Lord Keeper, Sir John Puckering, also was a tenant, so too was the Lord Chancellor Egerton whose tenancy is alluded to in the following letter from the Archbishop:

> I understand that your Lo. is desirous to be my tenant in my house near Charing Crosse. The trueth is that I was certainly informed that your Lo. had no inclination that way because the house standes nere the water and is thought to be somewhat rheumatike.[2]

Visscher's view shews the buildings near the river front. They have the appearance rather of a cluster of small houses than that of a Palace. The situation was near the position of the present Charing Cross Embankment Station, though not so near to the river. The Earl of Essex was there in 1592, apparently by the Queen's authority:

> Her Highness hath now committed the same unto the right honorable the Earle of Essex.[3]

In the time of his disgrace in 1599 he was under some

---
[1] So stated in Harben's *Dictionary of London*; not mentioned by Stow.
[2] 1596. To Sir Francis Egerton, *Egerton Papers*, 221.
[3] Norden's *Middlesex*, Harl. MS. 570 (Camden Society).

A LITERARY TOPOGRAPHY OF OLD LONDON

restraint. In November of that year a Royal Commission sat at Essex House, and Essex appeared to answer certain charges including alleged disobedience to the Queen's orders in Ireland, for which he was censured.[1] Sir Francis Bacon is seen again at York House at a later time in his career and appears to have possessed some rights of tenure. It is said that he was at York House in 1621 when he was compelled to give up the Great Seal. Only in the previous year, Bacon being then Viscount Verulam, Ben Jonson had eulogized him as the 'happy Genius of this ancient pile' (i.e. York House):

> Hail, happy Genius of this ancient pile!
> How comes it all things so about thee smile?
> The fire, the wine, the men! and in the midst
> Thou stand'st as if some mystery thou didst.
>
> . . . . . .
>
> 'Tis a brave cause of joy . . .
> Give me a deep-crowned bowl that I may sing,
> In raising him, the wisdom of my King.[2]

It is curious that as Henry VIII coveted Wolsey's York House, so James I coveted the second York Place. But it was not for himself. He wished to present it to his favourite Villiers, the first Duke of Buckingham, and he became the possessor in a legitimate way with fair compensation. Archbishop Laud has an entry in his Diary May 15, 1624:

> The Bill passed in Parliament for the King to have York-House in exchange for other Lands. This was for the Lord Duke of Buckingham.[3]

Henceforth York House had a new career under the Duke of Buckingham and his son the second Duke. The house was entirely rebuilt. Hollar's view (1630) shews a very large, plain and somewhat ugly building, having a long front to the river with monotonous rows of similar windows —not a very pleasing specimen of architecture, but it was a decadent age.[4]

---

[1] *Calendar of State Papers Domestic*, vol xxxiv. p. 399.
[2] 1620. On Lord Bacon's 60th birthday.
[3] Printed 1695, p 12.
[4] See view in Smith's *Antiquities of Westminster*.

YORK HOUSE, CHARING CROSS

There was a water-gate, said to be designed by Inigo Jones. This still stands *in situ* in the Gardens of the Thames Embankment and is a reminiscence of the last period of the greatness of the house of Villiers. It bears the family arms and their motto, '*Fidei coticula crux.*'[1]

The Duke spent vast sums of money in adorning his new mansion and filling it with pictures and works of art, but it was used mostly for state occasions, such as one described by Sir John Finett, Master of the Ceremonies in 1625:

> On Sunday the fifteenth of November the Duke of Buckingham having prepared a sumptuous entertainment of a supper and a maske at York-house for the French Ambassador Monsieur Bassompierre, had his Feast honored with the Presence of both their Majesties

The author takes occasion to remark 'how seriously the Queen was at that time applying herself to masks.'[2]

The first Duke did not long enjoy this kingly gift, for he was murdered in 1628. His son the second Duke, being then only one year old, could not have enjoyed his inheritance for many years, for the Civil War intervened before he arrived at manhood, and his estates were confiscated by the Parliament and York House was allotted to Lord Fairfax.

> He (i.e. Lord Fairfax) lived in York House where every Chamber was adorned with the Arms of Villiers and Manners, lions and peacocks He was descended from the same ancestors, earls of Rutland.[3]

There is an allusion to this in the 'Rump Songs':

> The house that lately great Buckingham's was
> Which now Sir Thomas Fairfax has
> Wish'd it might be Sir Thomas's fate so to passe.[4]

But a turn in the wheel of fortune brought York House back to its lawful owner. The Duke by marrying the daughter of Fairfax eventually became again the possessor

---

[1] The Cross, the Touchstone (or Whetstone) of Faith. Hollar's print may be seen in the Grangerized edition of Brayley's *London*, vol. iv. 433.
[2] *The Reception of Foreign Ambassadors* (1656), pp. 190 and 191.
[3] Brian Fairfax, *Memoirs of 2nd Duke of Buckingham, c.* 1699.
[4] *Rump Songs* (1662, p. 312). From MS. Arber, 1868.

of his paternal inheritance. The marriage, however, so it is said, nearly cost him his head, for Cromwell when he heard of it

rested not till he had him in the Tower and would have brought him to Tower Hill had he lived a fortnight longer.[1]

Evelyn says the House was in a neglected state in 1655.

I went to see York House and Garden belonging to the former greate Buckingham but now much ruin'd thro' neglect.[2]

In 1661 the Spanish Ambassador was there, and in 1663 the Russian Ambassador took up his residence there. So we gather from Samuel Pepys,[3] and we get the like information in Rugge's ' Mercurius Politicus Redivivus.'

Ten years after this the glory of York House had departed. In 1672 the Duke was tempted by a large offer to sell the estate for building purposes. The price is stated to have been £30,000. Streets were formed on the site of the house extending from the river front to the Strand. They bore the separate words of the Duke's name and title, and though the houses have been rebuilt the streets still retain the names. The desire of the Duke that his name should be thus perpetuated gave rise to a squib entitled ' The Duke of Buckingham's Litany ' :

> From calling streets by our own name
> When we've sold the land,
> *Libera nos, Domine.*

III

The house on the site of the old Temple in Holborn and known as ' Lincoln Place,' because occupied for a time by the Bishop of Lincoln, became afterwards the property of the Earls of Southampton, whose name still survives in Southampton Buildings.

The 30 July (1550) Sir Thos. Wriothesley Earle of Southampton, one of the Executors of King Henry VIII departed out of this transitory life at his place in Holborne called Lincolne Place . . . he was buried at S. Andrewes Church.[4]

---

[1] Fairfax Memoirs, as above   [2] *Diary*, Nov. 27, 1655.
[3] *Diary*, May 19, 1661, and June 6, 1663
[4] Wriothesley's *Chronicle*, 1550. Camden Soc. II. 41.

DORSET HOUSE

The place is best remembered in connexion with Henry Wriothesley, the friend and patron of Shakespeare.

Not far off, in Chancery Lane, was another Lincoln's Inn, so named after Henry Lacy, Earl of Lincoln. This in after years assumed a new character and is still famous as an 'Inn of Court.'

The Palace of the Bishop of Salisbury in Salisbury Square (Chap II.) was afterwards rented by the Sackville family and called Sackville House. Later on, when Lord Buckhurst became Earl of Dorset, the name was changed to 'Dorset House.' It was here that the tragedy *Ferrex and Porrex* was written by Thomas Sackville (afterwards the first Earl of Dorset). The play was also known as *Gorboduc*, the leading character, and was the first English tragedy written in blank verse. It was—to quote the title-page:

> shewed on stage before the Qveenes Maiestie the xviij day of Janvarie 1561, by the gentlemen of the Inner Temple.

Here died in 1652 Sir Edward Sackville, the fourth Earl of Dorset, a faithful adherent of Charles I in the Civil War.

Another of the King's staunch supporters, William Cavendish, Duke of Newcastle, who was much impoverished by the confiscation of his estates, seems to have had for a time the use of a portion of the house. Margaret, his second wife, in her life of her husband, wrote:

> After I was safely arrived in London I found my Lord in Lodgings . . . but soon after removed into Dorset House, which, though it was better than the former, yet not altogether to my satisfaction we having but a part of the said house in possession.[1]

Near by, between the Church of the White-friars and Fleet Street, in the 14th century was the house and grounds of Hugh Courtenay, Earl of Devon. He rebuilt the Church and was buried in the Choir.[2]

---

[1] *Life of William, Duke of Newcastle*, 1667 (1872, p. 112).
[2] The position is shewn in a plan of Whitefriars reproduced in Harben's *Dictionary of London*.

A LITERARY TOPOGRAPHY OF OLD LONDON

IV

The Bishop of Exeter's House (described elsewhere) became in after times known successively as 'Paget House,' 'Leicester House' and, best known of all, as 'Essex House,' the memory of which still survives in Essex Street, which marks the position.

> The same hath since been called Paget house because William Lord Paget enlarged and possessed it.[1]

This is the only mention of Paget House by Stow. William, first Baron Paget of Beaudesert, lived in the reign of Henry VIII He was mixed up with Queen Jane's party on the death of Edward VI, but notwithstanding we find him Lord Privy Seal under Queen Mary, an office which he resigned on the accession of Queen Elizabeth. He died in 1563 [2]

When Robert Dudley, Earl of Leicester, became possessor after Lord Paget he 'new builded there'—to use Stow's phrase Enlargement and adornment were no doubt necessary, for his Sovereign not only visited him but kept Court there. Sir Francis Walsingham enters in his Journal:

> Thursday, Feb. 27, 1577 The Queen's Majestie removed to Leicester House . . .
> Saturday, March 1. I went to the Court at Leicester House [3]

Sir Philip Sidney writes to his brother from Leicester House, October 18, 1580:

> Lord ! how I have bubbled : once again farewell dearest brother. Your most loving and careful brother.[4]

From the same place Edmund Spenser writes to Gabriel Harvey, October 5, 1579. 'The eternal memory of our

---
[1] Stow, *Survey* (1603), p. 446.
[2] See *Dict of Nat. Biog*
[3] *Journal* (1578), in Camden Miscellany, VI.
[4] *Miscell. Works* (1829), p 288.

ESSEX HOUSE

everlasting friendship.' Spenser has an allusion to Leicester House in his ' Prothalamion ' :

> Next whereunto [i.e. to the Temple]
> . . . . there standes a stately place
> Where oft I gayned giftes and goodly grace
> Of that great lord, which therein wont to dwell
> Whose want too well now feels my freendles case.

The Earl of Leicester left the house to his son-in-law, Robert Devereux, Earl of Essex, and thenceforward it was ' Essex House.' Spenser was not long ' friendless,' for a few lines further on in the poem (which was a ' Spousall Verse ' for a double wedding) we find him felicitating the new possessor on his victory in Spain:

> Yet therein now doth lodge a noble peer,
> Great England's glory, and the world's wide wonder
> Whose dreadfull name late through all Spaine did thunder.[1]

The poem was written in Essex House. Not long after this the Earl's prosperity and favour with Queen Elizabeth began to wane.

> The Quene is nothing satisfied with the Erle of Essex manner of proceeding. . . . The Quene is geven to understand that he hath geven Essex House to Antonie Bacon wherwith she is nothing pleased.[2]

On one side there was dissatisfaction and irritation, on the other pride and a sense of injury. Sympathizers with the Earl formed a faction. Sir James Whitelock alludes to

> the branesik meeting of the noblemen with the erl of Essex at Essex House on the 8 of February 1601.[3]

A writer hostile to Essex wrote at the time:

> Her Maiestie hauing understanding of this strange and tumultuous assembly at Essex House, yet in her princely wisdom and moderation thought to cast water upon the fire before it brake forth.[4]

The overt act of treason in attacking the City with an

[1] *Prothalamion*, l. 145 (1596).
[2] *Letter of John Chamberlain*, 1599 (Camden Soc., p 51).
[3] *Liber Famelicus*, c. 1609.
[4] *Declaration of the Treason of the E. of Essex* (1601, F.).

A LITERARY TOPOGRAPHY OF OLD LONDON

armed force and the fate of Essex are matters of history. Sir Robert Cecil, in a letter to Sir George Carew, describes the last stage.

> Being repulsed at Ludgate by a stand of pikes they ran for the water and put themselves into Essex House which the Earl had furnished with all manner of warlike provisions . . . the lady of Essex and Lady Rich were within it.[1]

In the time of the Rebellion we find Essex House in use by the Parliament for political purposes.

> They . . . gave directions that they [viz messengers from the King who had delivered his writs] should be tried by a Council of War as spies; which was done at Essex House.[2]

There was evidently a Chapel in the house as we read in Pepys' and Evelyn's Diaries after the Restoration that they attended service there.

Old plans shew the house as situate near the Strand, the space between it and the river being laid out as an Italian Garden [3]

Devereux Court in the Strand is still in evidence and a bust of Robert Devereux can still be seen there. This is not a portrait of Queen Elizabeth's favourite, but that of his son the third Earl, Parliamentary General in the Civil War.

A second Leicester House was so called from Sidney, Earl of Leicester by a second creation, and was situate in St. Martin's Lane, near Charing Cross. The house is alluded to in an anonymous tract published in 1641, the title of which is as follows·

> A Happy deliverance or a wonderfull preservation of four Worthy and Honorable Peeres of the Kingdom who should have been poysoyned at a supper in St Martin's Lane neere Charing-Crosse the 11 of Jan. 1641.

The Peers were the Earls of Leicester, Essex, Holland and Northumberland. The story is told by the cook, who avers that a Frenchman offered him £3000 to put poison

---
[1] *Carew Papers*, Feb 10, 1601.
[2] Clarendon, *Hist. of the Rebellion*, Bk. VII.
[3] See Smith's *Antiquities of Westminster*.

in the second course at supper. Leicester House was for a time the residence of Elizabeth, daughter of James I, the titular Queen of Bohemia, who died there in 1661.[1] In later years the house was used as a museum and contained the extensive natural history collection of Sir Ashton Lever. The existing Leicester Square occupies the site.

V

In the reign of Edward VI, Thomas Seymour, Baron Seymour of Sudeley and Lord High Admiral of England, following the method of his brother the Duke of Somerset in acquiring property, became the possessor of the Bishop of Bath's Palace [2] and it was known as Seymour Place. He married the Dowager Queen Katherine Parr, and on her death [3] was one of the many suitors of the Princess Elizabeth, who visited at the house and was offered the use of it when staying in London. At a later period he was executed for high treason (1549).

The house then passed into the hands of the Norfolk family. The young King Edward VI, who kept a Journal, makes this entry in the year 1548:

> The Earl of Arundel committed to his house for certain crimes of suspicion against him as plucking down of bolts and Locks at Westminster, giving of my Stuff away, etc.[4]

Robert Cary in his 'Memoirs' speaks of a 'keeper':

> My father having the keeping of Arundell House, I got lodging in it for myself, my wife and my servant.[5]

This was in the time of Philip, the first Earl of the Howard family, who was in the Tower, his offence being that he had had mass said for the success of the Spanish Armada.

---
[1] Pennant's *London*.
[2] Already dealt with under 'Bishops' Palaces.' 'Wrested' from the Bishop of Bath was Pennant's word.
[3] Some say 'before.'
[4] *Journal of Edward VI*, 1548.
[5] *c.* 1590 (1905, p. 37).

A LITERARY TOPOGRAPHY OF OLD LONDON

Edward Alleyn notes in his Diary his visit to Arundel House :

17 April 1618. I wase at Arundell Howse wher my Lord showed me all his statues and pictures that came from Italy.

As usual Alleyn enters his expenses :

giuen his man 0—2—0.[1]

This was Thomas Howard, the second Earl, famous as a collector. The marbles especially were in great repute and were presented to Oxford University in 1667. Two years before this the Earl had written to Alleyn, who had just opened his new College at Dulwich, asking him to ' accept of a poore fatherles boy.'[2]

In 1641 the Princess Mary, daughter of Charles I, was married, and the bridegroom, the Prince of Orange, was lodged at Arundel House.

Her Highnesse visited the Prince of Wales and Duke of York in Durham House which was returned by them at Arundell House the next day. The Prince every day saw the King and Queen and Princess having a key of the garden of Somerset House to come that way [3]

John Evelyn notes in his Diary, 25 May 1641 :

I sat to one Vanderborcht for my picture in oil at Arundel House.

He, Evelyn, was absent in Italy for some years during the troubles. After the Restoration he was instrumental in obtaining the gift of the fine Library at Arundel House to the Royal Society and of the marbles to Oxford. In 1666 he writes :

To the Royal Society which, since the sad conflagration, were invited by Mr. Howard to sit at Arundel House, who at my instigation, likewise bestowed on the Society that noble Library which his grandfather especially and his ancestors had collected

Another contemporary writer alludes to the books :

The Earl of Arundel's [Library] was the best for an Herald and an Antiquary, a Library not for shew, but use.[4]

---

[1] Dulwich MSS. No. IX. Catalogue, p. 170.   [2] *Ibid.* p. 101.
[3] *c* 1641. *Marriage of William, Prince of Orange*, Leland Miscell. Pieces, 1770, v. 337.
[4] 1670. David Lloyd, *State-Worthies*, p. 955.

ARUNDEL HOUSE

As to the marbles, a few months later he notes in his Diary:

> When I saw these precious monuments miserably neglected and scattered up and down about the garden and other parts of Arundel House and how exceedingly the corrosive air of London impaired them, I procured him to bestow them on the University of Oxford (Sept. 19, 1667).

Old plans which depict the house in its later period shew no signs of a stately mansion. The buildings are grouped round an open space and are small and in various styles, the whole giving somewhat the appearance of a well-kept country village and green.[1]

The connexion of the Norfolk family with the town of Arundel in Sussex has always existed. As an instance of theorising derivations it may be mentioned that Sir Thomas Elyot in his 'Boke called the Governour'[2] suggests a connexion with the somewhat mythical Bevis of Hampton:

> It is yet supposed that the Castell of Arundell in Sussex was made by one Beauvize erle of Southampton for a monument of his horse called Arundell which in ferre countrayes had saved his master from many perils.

The position of Arundel House is indicated by the modern streets, Norfolk Street, Arundel Street, Howard Street and Surrey Street, near the present Temple Station.

Richard FitzAlan, Earl of Arundel, in the reign of Richard II had a house in the older part of the City, being originally that of Sir John Pulteney. When the Earl was beheaded in 1397 his property fell to the King, and it seems a grant was made

> To the Knights John Bussy and Henry Grene of the stuff, utensils of the Hall etc. in the Inn in London late of Richard Earl of Arundel except silver vessels which belong to the King by forfeiture

Durham House, originally the Bishop's Palace, was converted by Henry VIII into a residence for Prince Edward.

---
[1] See Smith's *Antiquities of Westminster*.
[2] 1531, Bk I. xvij   The vale or dale of the river Arun is the more obvious derivation.

A LITERARY TOPOGRAPHY OF OLD LONDON

In the last days of King Edward VI the house was occupied by the Duke of Northumberland and, as Sir John Hayward relates,

> Whilest the King remained thus grievously sick, divers notable marriages were solemnized at Durham place. The Lord Guilford fourth sonne to the Duke of Northumberland married Lady Jane the Duke of Suffolkes eldest daughter.[1]

After her marriage the Lady Jane was entertained at Durham House, which was the rendezvous of the party desirous of placing her on the throne. Immediately after the death of the King in July 1553

> The Duke of Northumberland early in the morning called for all his owne harnes and sawe yt made redy. At Duram Place he apoynted all the retenue to mete[2]

Queen Elizabeth granted the House to Sir Henry Sidney, father of Sir Philip Sidney. Sir Henry, writing to Archbishop Parker, says:

> From Durham House the third of March 1567. The chiefest matter wherein I had to move your grace was for a licence to be granted to my boy Philip Sidney who is somewhat subject to sickness for eating of flesh in Lent.[3]

The use of the house was afterwards granted to Sir Walter Raleigh, who had it till after the death of Queen Elizabeth. John Chamberlain wrote in a letter:

> Sir W. Raleigh hath ben in Gersey . . . His lodgings at Durham House were almost burned the other day.[4]

In 1603 Sir Walter had notice to quit, at which he was somewhat indignant and wrote:

> I received warrant from your Lordshipps . . . requestinge me to deliver the possession of Derum howse to the Byshop of Derum before the xxiiijth day of June next insewinge (1603); this letter seemeth to me very strange seinge I have had the possession of the howse almost XX years and have bestowed well nere £2000 uppon the same.[5]

[1] *Life of Edward VI*, 1630 (1636, p. 415).
[2] *Chronicle of Queen Jane*, 1553 (1850, p. 60).
[3] *Parker Correspondence* (Parker Society), p. 316.
[4] 1600. *Letters* (Camden Society), p. 89.
[5] *Egerton Papers*, 380

DURHAM HOUSE

The case against Raleigh is stated in the arraignment:

> That the Lord Cobham did meet with the said Sir Walter Rawleigh . . . in Durham House . . . and then and there had conference with him how to advance Arabella Stewart to the Crowne and Royall Throne of this Kingdome.[1]

About the year 1640 the place was sold and the New Exchange built on a portion of the site. The following couplet is from the ' Rump Songs, 1653.' The occasion was the funeral of Admiral Deane, a Parliamentary General, somewhat a spectacular one with a procession by water:

> Th' Exchange and the ruines of Durham House eke
> Wish'd such sights might be seen each day o' th' week.[2]

A drawing by Hollar in 1630 gives a good idea of the House in his time. It appears to be built at the water's edge and has very small windows and something the appearance of a fortification.[3]

VI

The Bishop of Worcester's Place has already been noted as being destroyed when Somerset House was built. The house now to be considered is the home of the Earls of Worcester; but before touching upon this it will be convenient first to allude to the earlier house of the family (the only one mentioned by Stow) in the City, founded by John Tiptoft, the first Earl of Worcester, 1449. He was a man of good repute for his scholarship and of ill fame for his cruelty, having earned the title of ' the butcher of England.' He was a Yorkist and was executed on the fall of Edward IV. The house was in the neighbourhood of the Vintry, near St. James's, Garlick-Hythe. Stow

---

[1] *Arraignment and Conviction of Sir Walter Rawleigh*, 1603 (1648, p. 2).
[2] *Rump Songs* (1662), p 312.
[3] A model of the house as it appeared in 1650 after the New Exchange had been built on the Strand front, has been made by James P. Maginnis, A M I C.E., and may be seen at the London Museum. The Chapel may be seen with a lofty gabled roof and five Gothic windows on the north and south sides.

says 'in Anchor Lane.' An old London Directory has 'Worcester Place Lane,' and there is still 'Worcester Place.' The house seems to have been occupied by the Earl of Worcester till 1551, when he sold it.[1] In Stow's time

> diuided into many tenements. The fruiterers have their Hall there.[2]

A later writer says:

> The Fruiterers before the Fire had a part of Worcester House.[3]

Worcester House in the Strand was near Ivy Bridge and situate between the Savoy and Salisbury House. Pennant states (on the authority of Fuller) that this had originally been the residence of the Bishops of Carlisle. Of the several Earls of Worcester, Edward Somerset, sixth Earl and second Marquis, is worthy of note. He followed the King in the Civil War and suffered by his downfall, but recovered his estates at the Restoration. He devoted himself to scientific pursuits and curious inventions, and wrote a book well known to bibliophiles, 'The Century of Inventions.' Some of his ideas, though apparently impracticable, adumbrate important inventions of modern times. His son Henry became the first Duke of Beaufort —hence 'Beaufort House.' Edward Hyde, afterwards Lord Clarendon, lived there for some time, paying for it (according to Pennant) a rent of £500 a year, an enormous sum for that period. His daughter Anne married the Duke of York, afterwards James II. The wooing was romantic and took place abroad. The marriage was kept secret and celebrated privately at Breda, the Royal family being then in exile. This is James's own account:

> I was contracted to her on the 24th November 1659 at Breda in Brabant . . . and that we might observe all that is enjoyned by the Church of England I marned her upon the third of September last in the night between 11 and 12 at Worcester Houce my Chaplin Dr. Crowther performing that office . . . as is directed by the Book of Common Prayer . . . 18 Feb 1660 (Signed) James.[4]

[1] See note in Kingsford Edition of Stow.
[2] *Survey* (1603), p. 243.   [3] Cox, *Magna Britannia*
[4] Brit. Mus. MS. Additional No. 187470.

WORCESTER HOUSE

Dr. Crowther confirmed the above upon ' his corporate oath.'

Lord Clarendon lived for some few years at Worcester House, and in more prosperous times, after the Restoration, built himself a new mansion : but before that John Evelyn dined with him, as the latter relates in his Diary

> After dinner my Lord Chancellor and his lady carried me in their coach to see their palace (for he now lived at Worcester House in the Strand) building at the upper end of St James's Streete, and to project the garden.

It was probably soon after this that Clarendon wrote in his autobiography

> The meeting of the Persons the King appointed was at Worcester House [1]

Eventually the House was pulled down by the Beaufort family. Beaufort Buildings is in evidence

Hollar has a plate dated 1630 shewing Worcester House with the garden and a small water-gate.

VII

Stow places Bedford House next the Savoy, and assigns it in early times to the Bishop of Carlisle who, as already mentioned, lived there until he accepted Rochester House as an exchange.

> The Bishoppe of Carlile's Inne which now belongeth to the Earle of Bedford and called Russell or Bedford House It stretcheth west to Ivie Bridge.[2]

Machyn in his Diary fifty years earlier has :

> The xxx day of Marche (1554-5) the Earl of Bedford lord privy seal who died at his house beside the Savoy was carried to his burying place in the country called Chenies, with three hundred horse all in black.[3]

---

[1] *a* 1674, Edit. 1798, vol. iii. p. 217.
[2] *Survey* (1603), p. 449.
[3] H. Machyn, *Diary*, p. 83

A LITERARY TOPOGRAPHY OF OLD LONDON

Stow refers to this again in his MS. memoranda :

> Anno 1565. The King of Sweden's Systar cam to London and lodgyd at the Earle of Bedfords place at Yvebridge and was ther delyveryd of a male childe.

At a later period ' Bedford House ' was on the north side of the Strand. Little Bedford Street marks the position. Afterwards there was a Bedford House in Bloomsbury, built by Inigo Jones and at first known as Southampton House. Bedford Place marks the position. Evelyn records :

> Din'd at my Lo. Treasurer's the Earle of Southampton where he was building a noble square of piazza.[1]

In the last years of Queen Elizabeth, Sir Robert Cecil, Earl of Salisbury, the second son of the great Lord Burleigh, built his Mansion House adjoining Worcester House, and near to Ivy Bridge in the Strand. The existing Ivy Bridge Lane marks the position approximately. In 1602 he wrote to Sir George Carew :

> I have trymmed up a lodging for you in my new howse (called Cecyll howse) by Ivye bridge, from whence this letter is dated.[2]

The Bishop of London let him have some of the Caen stone which had been bought for the restoration of St. Paul's.[3] The house seems to have been enlarged about 1607, for we find :

> An Act for the assuring of certain small Parcels of ground to Robert Earl of Salisbury and his Heirs for the enlargement and commodious use of his Mansion House in the Strand now called Salisbury House and for recompence to be given for the same (3 James I).[4]

A view of the house by Hollar in 1630 shews it quadrangular in shape with corner turrets standing in the centre of a garden a short distance from the river, there being a water-gate and steps. A story is told of a tree in

---

[1] *Diary*, 1664–5, Feb 9.
[2] 1602, Oct. 24 (Camden Soc.), p. 144.
[3] *Hatfield Cal.*, xi. p. 36.
[4] *Journals of the House of Lords*, ii. 447

BURLEIGH HOUSE

the garden of Worcester House which obstructed the view and of Cecil's giving or offering to give £100 to get rid of it, with the result that the Earl of Worcester built up a wall.[1]

Sir Robert built Hatfield House (still the property of his successor), the estate having been taken by him in exchange for Theobalds, which the King much coveted and used frequently. Cecil, whom a contemporary writer describes as 'a true inheritor of his father's wisdom,' was the first Earl of Salisbury and a good friend to James before and after his accession, and the King much felt his loss. The writer above quoted describes the final interview :

> He took leave of the King who came to visit him at Salisbury House; and with tears at his parting protested to the Lords attending his great losse of the wisest Councellour and best servant that any Prince in Christendome could Paralel.[2]

There was an older Cecil House situate on the north side of the Strand, of which Stow writes :

> Sr Thomas Palmer in the reign of Edward VI began to build the same of brick but of later times it hath been far more beautifully increased by the late Sir William Cecill Baron of Burghley.[3]

This was the great Lord Burleigh the first Baron, Queen Elizabeth's Lord Treasurer, and the house became better known as 'Burleigh House.' It was built of brick with four square turrets, but did not enjoy so favourable a position as Sir Robert Cecil's house on the river front. There is an allusion to it in the Diary of J. Manningham in 1602 :

> Tarlton the Actor called Burley House-gate in the Strand towardes the Savoy the Lord Treasurer's Almes gate because it was seldom or never opened

When Burleigh died in 1598 the house came to his eldest son Thomas, the first Earl of Exeter, and thenceforward was known as Exeter House.

---

[1] A model of the two houses, 'Salisbury and Worcester,' as they appeared in 1650, has been prepared by Mr. James P. Maginnis, A.M.I.C.E., and may be seen in the London Museum.
[2] 1650. *Aulicus Coquinariæ, Court of James I*, p. 62.
[3] Stow, *Survey* (1603), p. 452.

A LITERARY TOPOGRAPHY OF OLD LONDON

In the time of James I the Spanish Ambassador was lodged there and entertained at the public expense—so it would seem from the following quotation:

He (i.e. the Spanish Ambassador) has cloths of estate at Exeter House, an honour never conceded to an Ambassador in Queen Elizabeth's time.[1]

Although the Ambassador was to be duly honoured, we see by a further entry that his entertainers 'had a frugal mind.'

The Council are going about to eat at Ordinaries, in order to choose which is fittest and cheapest to furnish diet for the expected Spanish Ambassador.

In later time the site was occupied by Exeter Change, an arcade with a gallery and shops and a show of tamed wild-beasts. The name of Exeter survived till the 19th century, when Exeter Hall had a considerable reputation and remained till our own time. An hotel now stands on the site, possessing nothing either in name or appearance to remind the casual visitor of Queen Elizabeth's greatest minister: but Burleigh Street near by is a reminiscence of the great statesman who once lived there.

VIII

According to Fuller,[2] Wimbledon House, close to Burleigh House, was begun in 1587 and finished in the next year by Sir Thomas Cecil; but Pennant has it that it was built by Edward Cecil, son to the first Earl of Exeter, who was created Viscount Wimbledon by Charles I. In 1628 (according to Baker's 'Chronicle'[3]):

There hapned a lamentable fire in the Strand which consumed Viscount Wimbledon's House (at that time) the lodging of the Dutch Embassador.

In the same year a portion of Wimbledon House at Wimbledon in Surrey was blown up by gunpowder.

[1] 1621, June 14, *Calendar of State Papers, James I (Domestic)*.
[2] *Church History* (1655), ix. 188.
[3] 1665, p. 496.

NORTHAMPTON HOUSE

Northampton House was built in 1614 by Henry Howard, Earl of Northampton, second son of Henry Howard, Earl of Surrey, the poet, upon the site (so Dugdale writes in his ' Monasticon ') and probably out of the ruins of the hospital of St. Mary Rouncival.[1] To use the words of another writer :

> He built the noble structure at Charing-Crosse from the ground, Northampton House, and presented it a New Year's gift to the Lord Walden Suffolkes eldest son [2] and now called Suffolk House.[3]

This is the third house bearing the name of Suffolk, two others having already been mentioned. It was the scene of the marriage of the Lady Margaret Howard, daughter of the Earl of Suffolk, the subject of a ballad by Sir John Suckling :

> At Charing Cross, hard by the way
> Where we, thou know'st, do sell our hay,
>   There is a house with stairs,
>   And there did I see coming down
> Such folk as are not in our town
>   Forty at least in pairs.[4]

According to another writer it was the munificence of King James that largely assisted in the erection of this fine mansion-house.

> He (King James) presented all, both Scottish and English, with Gifts, and those no small ones, for, by that the Earl of Northampton brother to Suffolk, had, he was alone able to raise and finish the goodly pile he built in the Strand which yet remains a monument.[5]

At a later date it became by marriage the property of Algernon, Earl of Northumberland, and thenceforward was known as Northumberland House.

---

[1] *Op. cit.*, Edit 1846, iv. pt ii. p 677.
[2] This was Theophilus Howard, second Earl of Suffolk. He was Lord Warden of the Cinque Ports in 1628.
[3] *Aulicus Coquinariæ* (1650), p. 66. See also W. Sanderson, *Reign of James I* (1656), p. 394.
[4] *a* 1640 The present Suffolk Place is close to the Haymarket.
[5] Fr. Osborne, *Memoirs, King James* (1658), *Works* (1673), p 472.

A LITERARY TOPOGRAPHY OF OLD LONDON

John Evelyn was a visitor there, and mentions the stairs alluded to in Suckling's poem already quoted:

> I went to see the Earl of Northumberland's pictures ... the new front towards ye gardens is tolerable were it not drown'd by a too massive and clumssie pair of stayres of stone without any neate invention.[1]

It would appear that the whole of the land in the rear had not (at all events in Evelyn's time) been acquired, as he speaks of smoke nuisance and mean buildings adjacent to the house:

> I have strangely wondred ... when the south-wind has been gently breathing to have sometimes beheld that stately House and garden belonging to my Lord of Northumberland wrapped in a horrid cloud of smoake issuing from a Brew-house or two contiguous to that noble Palace.[2]

Evelyn, in the work just cited, describes the smoke-nuisance in London in the reign of Charles II as serious.

Northumberland House stood till the latter part of the last century. Northumberland Avenue marks the position approximately.[3]

The old residence of the Percy family, dating from the 14th century, was close to Saint Martin-le-grand. One great house, so Stow writes, belonging to Henry Percy, but —so he continues—

> King H. the 4 in the 7 of his reign gave this house ... to Queene Jane his wife and then it was called her wardrope—it is now a Printing House.[4]

---

[1] *Diary*, June 9, 1658

[2] Evelyn, *Fumifugium* (1661), p. 7.

[3] An excellent model of this house, as it was supposed to have appeared in 1650, has been executed by J. P. Maginnis, A.M.I.C.E., and may be seen at the London Museum. The plan of the building is a hollow square, the mansion having four towers with cupolas. The windows and gables have the character of the Tudor period, but the upper storeys of the towers have round-headed and circular windows.

[4] *Survey* (1603), p. 311. Mr. Kingsford in his edition of Stow has a note that Henry Percy, the first Earl, gave it to his son Harry Hotspur. Both father and son were in rebellion and defeated and killed in battle. This accounts for the house being in possession of the King.

SIR ROBERT COTTON'S HOUSE

This, the King's Printing House, was afterwards moved to Blackfriars.[1] After several ownerships, the Percys were again in possession of the house in 1557 and remained owners till 1607, when it was sold. In Agas's Map of London it is clearly shewn, close to the City wall in Aldersgate Street, and appears to stand on a large site extending nearly as far back as the 'Grey Friars.'

Near by in Aldersgate Street Shaftesbury Court marks the position of the house of Anthony Ashley Cooper, Earl of Shaftesbury. The house has been removed. The London Lying-in Hospital took its place.

The Percys at a later period had another Northumberland House situate in Fenchurch Street near to Aldgate. Stow writes of this that it

belonged to Henrie Percie Earle of Northumberland in the three and thirtie of Henrie the Sixt (1455) but of late being left by the Earles the Gardens thereof were made into Bowling Alleys and other parts into dicing houses, etc.[2]

IX

Another house at Westminster is worthy of notice, not so much for its size or princely magnificence, but for its interesting associations. Sir Robert Cotton's house would appear to have been, at all events in part, a portion of the old Palace, indeed the Library is said to have been the Oratory of Edward the Confessor, which probably is identical with the Chapel of St. John the Evangelist. Its position was near the river adjoining the Speaker's garden.[3] Another writer says 'in the passage out of Westminster Hall into the Old Palace Yard a little beyond the stairs going up to St. Stephen's Chapel.'[4]

[1] The King's printer in the time of James I was Robert Barker, who produced the Folio Bible of 1611, in our time called 'the Authorized Version.'
[2] Stow's *Survey* (1603), p. 151.
[3] Smith's *Antiquities of Westminster*.
[4] N Bailey's *Hist. of London*

A LITERARY TOPOGRAPHY OF OLD LONDON

According to Camden the Confessor died not in but in some place adjacent to Cotton House.

> This religious and good King died at Westminster, the Chamber wher he died yet remaineth close to Sir Thomas Cotten's house.[1]

During the trial of King Charles I at Westminster Hall the King spent the nights at Cotton House.

> The next day the King was in a Sedan or close chair removed from Whitehall to Sir Robert Cotton's house—Guards were made on both sides King Street [2]

Clarendon says:

> The King . . . went not to bed by reason the soldiers guarded all night in the same room with their swords drawn.[3]

Sir Robert Cotton is best remembered in our day for the fine collection of books and MSS. now in the British Museum. The Collection remained at Cotton House for two generations, and we find Bishop Burnet complaining that he could not get access. He writes:

> I got for some days into the Cotton Library But Duke Lauderdale . . got Dolben Bishop of Rochester to divert Sir John Cotton from suffering me to search into his library [4]

Sir John was the grandson of Sir Robert, and he it was who gave the collection to the nation.

Goring House was the residence of Baron Goring, Earl of Norwich, and stood where Buckingham Palace now stands. Dorothy Osborne mentions it in a letter to Sir William Temple:

> I will begin my story as you did yours from our parting at Goring House.[5]

Samuel Pepys took his wife there:

> Home and called my wife and took her . . . to a great wedding at Goring House . . . But of all the beauties there my wife was thought the greatest [6]

---

[1] Camden's *Remains Concerning Britain* (1605). Sir Thomas was the son of Sir Robert

[2] Jan. 1648. Sir Thos. Herbert, *Memoirs of Charles I*. At this time Sir Thomas, son of Sir Robert, was the owner

[3] Clarendon, *State Papers*, II Appendix li.

[4] *History of his own Time*, 1676.

[5] 1653. Letter 3.

[6] *Diary*, July 10, 1660.

HATTON HOUSE

Subsequently it became the property of the Earl of Arlington, a member of the *Cabal*. It was sold to John Sheffield, Duke of Buckingham, who obtained more land and built a new mansion in Queen Anne's reign, known as Buckingham House.

Hatton House in Holborn was built by Sir Christopher Hatton on the orchard and garden of Ely House adjacent, the Bishop of Ely under pressure from Queen Elizabeth having given it up, as already noted. In the early years of the reign of Charles I Hatton House was sometimes used for rehearsals of the Court Masques. James Shirley, in his Preface to 'The Triumph of Peace,' 'The Masque of the gentlemen of the four honorable Societies or Inns of Court,' goes on to say :

At Ely and Hatton Houses, the gentlemen and their assistants met and . . . prepared for the Court.

This was performed before the King and Queen at the Banqueting House, Whitehall, the Queen and the ladies of the Court joining in the dances. The production was carried out with the most extravagant magnificence and is said to have cost £21,000. Inigo Jones designed the scenes and William Lawes and Simon Ives wrote the music, 'whose art gave an harmonious soul to the otherwise languishing numbers.'[1]

Stow does not mention Hatton House in his 'Survey,' but he humorously alludes to the Monument in St. Paul's, near to those of Sir Philip Sidney and Sir Francis Walsingham :

> Philip and Francis have no tombe
> For great Christopher takes all the roome.

The site known as Hatton Garden marks the position of his house.

A short distance to the west, Brooke Street, Holborn, remains in evidence of the residence of Sir Fulke Greville, Lord Brooke, 'the friend of Sir Philip Sidney' (as he liked to call himself) and his biographer. The owner of

---

[1] *Triumph of Peace*, Jas. Shirley, 1633.

the house met with his death by violence on September 30, 1628. It

was occasioned by the rage of one Haywood who having been the greater part of his life in his service and thinking himself not sufficiently rewarded, gave him a mortal stab in the back . . . in his bed-chamber at Brooke House Holbourne.[1]

In the reign of Charles II ·

The Committee—named to examine the accounts of the money that was given during the Dutch War . . . because it sat in Brook House was called by the name of that house (1668).[2]

Near by was the mansion of Sir William Furnival, afterwards an Inn of Chancery and now absorbed by the Prudential Insurance Company Close at hand was the Earl of Bath's Place. Stow writes · ' the Earle of Bathe's Inne . . of late for the most part new builded.'[3]

Some little distance to the west, and on the north side of the Oxford Road, stood in ancient times the Manor House of Tottenhall, in later times Tottenham Court. It dated from the 11th century if not earlier, and is mentioned in Domesday Book :

The Canons of St. Paul's hold Totenhele [4]

In the time of Queen Elizabeth the Manor was with the Crown and so remained for many years. In the 17th century it became the property of the Fitzroy family and eventually Fitzroy Square was built on a portion of the land. The house was converted into a tavern known as the ' Adam and Eve ' and was popular as a pleasure resort. There were tea gardens offering an additional attraction. Tottenham Court Road remains a reminiscence.

The house already alluded to as Carlisle House, and situated in Lincoln's Inn Fields at the corner of Queen Street, seems to have been burnt down about 1684 and was rebuilt in 1686 by William Herbert, first Viscount Powis,

[1] T. Birch, *Memoirs, Q. Elizabeth* (1754), p 179
[2] Burnet's *Hist. of his own Time* (1724), p. 268.
[3] Stow's *Survey* (1603), p. 390
[4] Brit. Mus. trans. of Middlesex in *Domesday*, p. 11

WARWICK HOUSE

an adherent of James II and imprisoned in the Tower for alleged complicity in the so-called Popish Plot. The house then fell to the Crown, and afterwards became the property of the Duke of Newcastle [1] and bore his name. It still stands, the Queen Street front extending over the footpath and supported on arches.

An older house remains. This is Lindsey House (on the west side of the Square). It was built by Inigo Jones, who wished, so it is said, that the whole Square should be carried out in the same style. The Earl of Lindsey who first occupied it was killed at Edgehill in 1642.[2]

The earliest house built by the Earl of Warwick was in Eldenese Lane, Newgate Street,[3] adjacent to the Church of St. Ewin. Stow alludes to this as ' Warwicke Inne, an ancient house builded by an Earle of Warwicke ... the 28 of Henry the 6 Cicille Dutches of Warwicke possessed it.'[4] Stow appears to refer to Richard Neville, Earl of Warwick, ' the King Maker.'[5] In the reign of Charles I there was a Warwick House in Holbourne. Arthur Wilson stayed there, and relates a misadventure in the street:

> The same winter (1633) being at Warwick House my Charitie expos'd me to a durty hazard. For a good comely well cloth'd man falling downe in the street by mee, I ventur'd to help him up. The man being drunk flew about my ears swearing I threwe him downe and though I shunn'd his embrace yet was I soild with his durt. Soe dangerous is it often time to be charitable.[6]

The present Warwick Court indicates the position.

[1] Thornbury's *London*, iii. 47. Thornbury says he was the father of the Countess of Nithsdale, who effected the escape of her husband from the Tower by a change of dress.
[2] In modern times John Forster lived there, and was visited by Charles Dickens, who probably had it in mind when he introduced his readers to Mr. Tulkinghorn in *Bleak House*.
[3] Mr. Kingsford derives ' Eldeness Lane' from ' Old Dean's Lane.'
[4] *Survey* (1603), p. 345.
[5] A writer in the *Gentleman's Magazine* (1820) says: ' His statue is now in a house there.' This is referred to by Pennant as the statue of Guy, Earl of Warwick, whose fame is in the old romance bearing his name. There is still to be seen a sculptured effigy on the house at the corner of Newgate Street. It is dated 1668.
[6] *a.* 1652. *Observations of God's Providence* (1814, p. 129).

According to Pepys it was occupied by Lord Manchester in 1659-60:

> After dinner I to Warwick House in Holborne to my Lord, where he dined with my Lord of Manchester. I staid in the great Hall [1]

Southampton House has already been alluded to under the heading of the Bishop of Lincoln's house. It was the town mansion of the Wriothesley family, Earls of Southampton. Pennant wrote that in his time the 'King's Head' tavern was the only part of it remaining.

In 1581 the Recorder of London was ordered

> to resort unto the Earle of Southamton's howse in Holborne and there to make search for the apprehending of one William Spencer noated unto their Lordships to be a very badd fellow and practising against the State . . also to searche the said howse for bookes letters and ornaments for massinge [2]

The house is alluded to in a play by Mrs. Aphra Behn:

> Meet me tomorrow morning about 5 with your sword in your hand behind Southampton House.[3]

Near by lived John Gerard, the herbalist. Probably the house was no mansion, and Stow, who was his contemporary, does not mention it, but the garden acquired great fame, and Gerard published a list of plants therein which was the first catalogue of the kind. His best known work was the 'Herball' (1597).

X

Drury Lane, connecting the Strand with St. Giles's, is shewn in old maps as a country lane having no houses save the large mansion, the seat of the Drury family.[4]

---

[1] *Diary*, Mar. 3, 1659-60. From the date this would appear to refer to Edward Montagu, second Earl of Manchester.
Another Earl of Warwick, Robert Rich, Earl of Warwick and Holland, is said to have had a house in 'Cloth Fair,' West Smithfield, and his arms are said to have still been affixed to a shop in 1795. See *Gentleman's Magazine* (1795), part iii. p. 810.

[2] *Acts of the Privy Council*, vol. 13, p. 298.

[3] 1677. *The Town Fopp*, I. ii.

[4] The earliest mention of the family in the *Dict. of Nat. Biog.* is Sir Robert Drury, who was Speaker of the House of Commons in 1495.

DRURY HOUSE

There were frequent references to the house in connexion with the Essex Rebellion, as the adherents of the Earl used to meet there. A tract of the time reads:

> And because hee thought himselfe and his own house more obscrued, it was thought fit that the meeting and conference should bee at Drury House, where Charles Dauers lodged [1]

Sir Richard Baker denies that the consultations at Drury House were treasonable

> And for the consultations in Drury House it is no more to be called High Treason then an Embryon may be accounted a perfect man [2]

Sir Robert Cecil in a letter to Sir George Carew alludes to 'the conspirascies that were at Drury Howse' and pities

> the poore yong Erle of Southampton who meerly for the loue of the Erle hath ben drawen into this action [3]

In Isaak Walton's 'Life of Dr. Donne' we read:

> Sir Robert Drury a gentleman of a very noble estate and more liberal mind assigned him (Dr Donne) and his wife an useful apartment in his own large house in Drury Lane

It was Elizabeth Drury the daughter who died at the age of fifteen of whom Donne wrote:

> One whose clear body was so pure and thin
> Because it need disguise no thought within

This is from one of many elegies on this young lady.[4]

Sir Richard Weston, Chancellor of the Exchequer, was living in Drury Lane (but whether in Drury House or elsewhere does not appear) in the reign of Charles I, as is seen from an entry in the 'Remembrancia' of the City of London:

> 8 May 1627. An order of the Court of Aldermen granting during pleasure to Sir Richard Weston, Knight, Chancellor of the Exchequer, a quill of water from the City's main pipe to serve his necessary use at his house in Drury Lane.[5]

---

[1] 1601. *Declaration of the Treason of the late E. of Essex*, D. 4. Dauers (or Danvers) was executed for complicity.
[2] *Chronicle*, 1643 (Elizabeth, p 109)
[3] 1600 Camden Soc., p. 74
[4] See Sir Ed Gosse, *Life of Donne*, i. 274.
[5] *Op. cit.* vi. 99 Index, 558.

A LITERARY TOPOGRAPHY OF OLD LONDON

Drury House in later years became the residence of the Earl of Craven, and was known for a time as Craven House. William, the first Earl of Craven, rebuilt the house and was living there at or soon after the Restoration, and he offered the use of it to Elizabeth, Queen of Bohemia, in 1661,[1] in which year Thomas Rugge, a contemporary journalist, writes:

> August. The Queen of Bohemia still remains at Drury House, and is very much visited by our English ladies and she is very much honoured and beloved of all sorts of people.[2]

In the same year Dorothy Osborne was staying there.[3] The Earl took a great interest in fires, especially after the great conflagration of 1666.[4]

Wallingford House was situate near the Horse-guards, and was so named from Sir William Knollys, Earl of Banbury and Viscount Wallingford (1616). The first Duke of Buckingham bought the house, and his son the second Duke was born there. The following quotation from one of Wotton's letters is interesting as it indicates that in the time of the Stuarts such important posts as the Provostship of Eton and the Mastership of the Rolls could be obtained by purchase:

> I had under his own royal hand (James I) two hopes in reversion. The first a moiety of the six Clerks' place in Chancery. The next the office of the Rolls itself. The first of these I was forced to yield to Sir Willm Beecher ... and that was as much in value as my Provostship were worth at a market. The other of the reversion of the Rolls I surrendered to the said Duke (of Buckingham) in the gallery at Wallingford House.[5]

It would appear from another letter of Sir Henry Wotton that Sir Richard Weston, first Earl of Portland and Lord

---

[1] At a later period there was a tavern near by having the sign of 'The Queen of Bohemia's Head.' The Earl is said to have been privately married to the Queen, but there is little probability in the story It is, however, stated as a fact by a writer in the *Gentleman's Magazine*, 1820.
[2] *Collection of most Material Occurrences*, B.M. Addit. MSS.
[3] See *Letter to Sir W. Temple*.
[4] See a letter of Charles Hatton in 1676, Camden Society (1878), p. 140.
[5] Feb. 12, 1628–9, *Letters* (1907), vol. ii. p. 315.

WALLINGFORD HOUSE

Treasurer, was living there in 1635. This was the year of his death.

> On Friday (Mar. 12, 1635) coming homewards from Wallingford House, where I had been to attend my Lord Treasurer's leisure and health, etc.[1]

The house was opposite the Banqueting Hall, and it is said that from the roof Archbishop Ussher witnessed the last scene on the scaffold at the execution of Charles I.,

In the year before the Restoration, the Committee of Safety was located there—as we read in a letter dated May 10, 1659, addressed to General Monk and signed by Lambert, Vane and others, signifying their appointment as a Committee.[2] Another letter, Nov. 29, 1659, alludes to this:

> Wallingford House say that the Council of State have mete severall tymes to rayse forces and plott to destroy the godly, forsooth.[3]

The following excerpts are all dated 1659:

> I went to Lieut. General Fleetwood who endeavoured to persuade me to go in to a council of officers that were then assembled at Wallingford House to consider letters brought from Col. Monk.[4]

In the 'Memoirs' of Colonel Hutchinson we read:

> After that [the Committee of Safety] setting up their army Court at Wallingford House, they began their arbitrary reign to the joy of all the vanquished enemies of the parliament.[5]

The following is the title of a pamphlet of eight pages:

> 'The Soldiers' publick Library, lately erected for the benefit of all that love the good old Cause at Wallingford House.'

The following is from a letter of Lord Chancellor Hyde, afterwards Earl of Clarendon:

> The City on Tuesday last (Dec. 27) shut their gates and fell upon the Council at Wallingford House and drove all the soldiers out of town—what they will do next we cannot be long without knowing.[6]

[1] *Letters* (1907), ii. 351.
[2] Camden Society, *Clarke Papers*, iv. 120. [3] *Ibid.* p. 300.
[4] *Memoirs of Gen. Ludlow* (Parliamentary Army), Oct. 29, 1659 (1894, ii. 132).
[5] *Op. cit*, edit. 1846, p. 387.
[6] To Sir H. Bennett. *Clarendon State Papers*, vol. iii. p. 636.

A LITERARY TOPOGRAPHY OF OLD LONDON

At the Restoration, George Villiers, the second Duke of Buckingham, was restored to his confiscated estates. His biographer Bryan Fairfax writes of him as being at Wallingford House:

> At the King's Coronation no subject appeared in greater splendour: none kept greater hospitality than he did at Wallingford House, specially for the French nobility that came over [1]

Lord Clarendon, at the height of his prosperity, built a large mansion in Piccadilly, nearly opposite St. James's Street. As Burnet wrote, at or soon after the time:

> The King (Charles II) had granted him a large piece of ground near S James's to build a house on ... he put the managing into the hands of others, who ran him to a vast charge of about fifty thousand pounds Some called it Dunkirk House intimating that it was built by his share of the price of Dunkirk (1667) [2]

Andrew Marvell, no friend to Clarendon, has a satire entitled 'Clarendon's House-warming,' from which two lines may be cited·

> He begged for a palace so much of his ground
> As might carry the measure and name of a Hyde.[3]

The house was one of the largest in London, and some indignation was roused by the extravagant expense. It was said that stone was used that had been provided for the repair of Old St. Paul's, and Marvell wrote an epigram:

> Here lie the sacred bones
> Of Paul deprived of his stones.

But the story of the stones was also related of Sir Robert Cecil when he built his house. As a matter of fact the material was purchased *bona fide* by Lord Clarendon.[4] The site of the house was unusually large for any private

---

[1] Bryan Fairfax, *Memoirs of D of Buckingham.* See Arber's reprint of the *Rehearsal* (Preface).
[2] *History of his own Time*, B ii (1724, p. 249).
[3] Marvell's pun on the family name of Hyde is rather extravagant: a hide of land is about 100 acres Clarendon carried out the sale of Dunkirk though he did not initiate it. See *Dict of Nat. Biog.*
[4] See Pennant's *London.*

CLARENDON HOUSE

mansion in such a position. A contemporary diarist writes that 8 acres were enclosed.

> In the month of August 1664 over against S. James's House, the foundations laid and wall made that rounded eight acres of ground for the intended house built by the Lord Chancellor.[1]

The cost, much larger than he intended, caused Lord Clarendon much embarrassment. He mortgaged the property to the Earl of Burlington for £10,000, and after his death it was sold to Christopher, Duke of Albemarle, for £25,000, a sum apparently below its value, and was thenceforth known as Albemarle House. Albemarle Street is a reminiscence.

George Monk, Duke of Albemarle, was succeeded by James, Duke of Ormond. The house had but a brief career, for in 1683 it was demolished by Sir Thomas Bond and the existing Bond Street was constructed on the site.

Sir John Berkeley of Bruton, afterwards Earl Berkeley of Stratton, built the house in Piccadilly bearing his name. The house is figured in the map of Ogilvie and Morgan, 1682. It was somewhat imposing in appearance, the façade having wings in advance of the main building.

> One of the most magnificent pallaces of the towne

was Evelyn's comment in his 'Life of Mrs. Godolphin,'[2] who stayed there for a time. The house afterwards became the property of the Duke of Devonshire, who built a new house on a portion of the site. The present streets, John Street, Bruton Street, Stratton Place, Hay Street, are all reminiscences of the Berkeley family, dating from the 11th century, whose ancient mansion known as 'Barklies Inne,' though in ruins, was still standing in Stow's time in Thames Street, near to Puddle Dock, with the family arms carved thereon.

There was yet another Berkeley House in Clerkenwell near St. John's Lane and Berkeley Street (also called Bartlett Street). It is described as a spacious mansion

---
[1] Thos. Rugge, *Mercurius Politicus Redivivus*
[2] First published in 1847. See also Evelyn's *Diary*, Sept. 25, 1672.

flanked by two wings, having a courtyard and a garden. This was the residence of Sir Maurice Berkeley, said to have been standard-bearer to Henry VIII, Edward VI, and Queen Elizabeth.[1] At a later date George, Lord Berkeley, known as 'George the Traveller,' had it. In his youth he had for tutor Philemon Holland, well known as the translator of Pliny, Plutarch and Camden's 'Britannia.'[2]

The present Devonshire Square in Bishopsgate Street marks the site of what was once the residence of William Cavendish, Earl of Devonshire. But it had many previous owners and occupiers, the Earl of Oxford being one. It is even said that Queen Elizabeth, whose brief and rapid visitation of her subjects has been already mentioned, was lodged there. But the house was best known and commented on as 'Fisher's Folly,' from the name of the original builder

> It is, sir, a verie faire house indeede . . . builded by one Jasper Fisher free of the Goldsmithes.[3]

Fisher was one of the six Clerks of the Chancery. Stow describes the house as:

> Large and beautifull with gardens of pleasure, bowling alleys and such like . . . large and sumptuous but built by a man of no great calling[4]

In fact, the great cost of so extensive a mansion was far beyond the means of the builder, and the unfortunate Jasper was much in debt. Hence the nickname, given in ridicule but surviving for several generations in spite of noble owners It became a byeword to give point to a satire. The following is from a Broadside printed in 1660 just after the Restoration, when General Monk was the popular hero:

> The Entertainment of Lady Monk at Fisher's Folly with an addresse made to her by a member of the Colledge of Bedlam at her visiting those Phanatiques.

---

[1] The second wife of Sir Maurice was Lady Elizabeth Berkeley, who died in 1585 and was buried in the Church of St James, Clerkenwell. See Brayley's *Londiniana*, vol. 1. 148.
[2] See Pink's *History of Clerkenwell* This Sir Maurice is not mentioned by Stow, nor is he given in the *Dict of Nat Biog*.
[3] *Pleasant Walks of Moore fields*, Rich. Johnson, 1607.
[4] *Survey* (1603), p 167

FISHER'S FOLLY

This is from the supposed speech of the Bedlamites:

> Our Bedlam true Phanatiques keep
> Not such as dream when fast asleep
> Let George know we are not so mad
> But we can love an honest lad [1]

In the following the author of 'Hudibras' is satirising a packed Parliament.

>   members
> That represent no part of th' nation
> But Fisher's Folly congregation [2]

The house, or some part of it, was eventually used as a Meeting House presided over by William Kiffen, a Baptist of the sect known as Independents.[3]

It will be seen that the name of Fisher's Folly was still in use after the Restoration when the King honoured the old Countess with a visit. A contemporary diarist writes:

> November 1660 The King, Queen, Duke of York and the rest of the Royal family supped at 'Fisher's Folly' at the old Countess of Devonshire's.[4]

Another possible Devonshire House, at an earlier date, is indicated in the following quotation:

> I showd to Ed. [de la Pole] that I understode by the said Huse that to litil afore his departing he shuld have dynyd in Warwik Lane witherl of Devonshire and that therle cam unto his uttre jayet to receif hym.[5]

Warwick House has already been mentioned. Edward Courtenay was Earl of Devonshire in 1503 [6] and might also have had a house in Warwick Lane or might have had the use of Warwick House. It is worth noting that in the list of monuments mentioned by Stow in the old church of the Grey Friars (Christ Church) which was close by, the

---

[1] From J P Collier's Reprints
[2] Butler's *Hudibras*, 3rd Part, Canto ii
[3] See *Ancient Meeting Houses*, G H. Pike, p. 2.
[4] Thos Rugge, *Mercurius Politicus Redivivus*
[5] 'Deposition touching Edmund de la Pole' in *Letters and Papers Henry VII*, 1503, 226 Devonshire House in Piccadilly belongs to a much later period.
[6] *Dict of Nat. Biog.*

A LITERARY TOPOGRAPHY OF OLD LONDON

name appears of 'Margaret de Rivers, Countess of Devon.' No date is given.[1]

Yet another Warwick House is heard of as being in Cloth Fair near Bartholomew Close, and said to have been still standing at the close of the last century, and to have been the residence of Robert, Earl of Warwick, Parliamentary General, who acquired it from his ancestor Sir Robert Rich.[2]

Near the Charterhouse in Aldersgate Street was Rutland House. The following allusion is of interest, shewing the production of a play with the addition of music four years before the Restoration. It seems a room had been built at the back of the house and used as a theatre. Here was performed on May 23, 1656

a piece entitled 'The first day's Entertainment' by Sir William Davenant.

described as being

by Declamation and Musick after the manner of the ancients.

Songs by Henry Lawes and Dr. Coleman were introduced.[3]

XI

Although not in London or Westminster, Kensington being a suburb, brief mention must be made of two houses, each a fine specimen of the Elizabethan period of architecture. Holland House is fortunately still with us, a typical specimen of Tudor domestic Gothic; one of the finest mansion-houses of its own period and the only perfect specimen of that period now remaining in London. Sir Walter Cope, Chamberlain of the Exchequer (1609), built it in 1607 and named it (or it was so called) Cope Castle. He bequeathed the property to his son-in-law Henry Rich, first Earl of Holland. Lord Holland was in favour with

---
[1] Stow, *Survey* (1603), p. 322.
[2] See Brayley's *Londiniana*, ii. 192.
[3] *Cal. of State Papers, Interregnum*, vol. 128, f. 352. See also Pepys Club Papers, i. 131.

HOLLAND HOUSE

James I, and was employed in the negotiations for the French marriage of Charles I. He took the King's part at the commencement of the Civil War, but changed sides more than once, though he was on the Royalist side when captured at St. Neots and was executed. After his death Holland House was occupied by Fairfax. A journal of the day states:

> The Lord General is removing from Queen Street to the late Earl of Holland's House at Kensington.[1]

It was a coincidence that the wife of Fairfax was of the Vere family (Earls of Oxford) who were the original owners of the estate sold to Sir Walter Cope.

The Fairfax occupation of Holland House was not a lengthy one, as the Countess with her children was allowed quiet repossession. It should be noted that the first Earl of Holland was the younger son of Robert Rich, first Earl of Warwick (hence the conjunction of the two titles hereafter) His mother was Penelope, daughter of Robert Devereux, Earl of Essex, said to have been the 'Stella' of Sir Philip Sidney. Before the Civil War there were many visitors Amongst others the French Ambassador Bassompierre, who kept a diary, in which is the entry[2]:

> Le mercredi 25. Je fus dîner chez le Comte de Hollande à Stintinton.

For many years Holland House was let by the family to a succession of tenants. William III is said to have contemplated taking it. In the next century, which does not fall within the period allotted to this work, it became the residence of Joseph Addison, who had married the Dowager Countess of Warwick and Holland. It was there that he died. An enthusiastic modern writer says 'His death in it is its greatest event.'[3]

In the vicinity of Holland House was another fine specimen of the Tudor mansion, though on a smaller scale.

---
[1] See Leigh Hunt's *Memorials of Kensington*, i. 281.
[2] See Leigh Hunt, *The Old Court Suburb*, 1. 280.
[3] Leigh Hunt.

A LITERARY TOPOGRAPHY OF OLD LONDON

It was built about 1612 by Sir Baptist Hicks, one of James the First's baronets, whom he afterwards created Viscount Campden of Campden in Gloucestershire. Sir Baptist Hicks was well known in the City as a wealthy silk mercer of Cheapside, who built a Hall called by his name on the site of what is now the Clerkenwell Sessions House. His only child, a daughter, inherited the property and title and married Edward Noel, of a Rutland family, who became the second Viscount Campden. His son, named Baptist from his grandfather, was the third Viscount, and during the Commonwealth in 1645 was obliged to compound with the Commissioners of Sequestration, who for a time took the house for their own use. Thomas Rugge in 'Mercurius Politicus Redivivus' has an allusion to Camden House (presumably meaning Campden).

> 1660, 13 September. The Ambassador Extraordinary of the King of Spain, Prince de Ligne, came into London very nobly attended. He lay at Camden House, and kept a noble table for all persons of quality of our English nation.[1]

At the latter end of the century it was for a time let to the Princess Anne, afterwards Queen, who with her husband Prince George of Denmark spent part of their time there. The house remained till 1862, when it was burnt down. 'Campden House' in Maiden Lane, Aldersgate Street, received its name from the second Viscount, Sir Edward Noel, who rented it from the Goldsmiths' Company about 1630.

[1] See *Gentleman's Magazine*, 1852, part ii. p. 47.

CHAPTER IV

Some Mansion-houses of Eminent Citizens, within the City and Eastward of St. Paul's

CHAPTER IV

Some Mansion-houses of Eminent Citizens, within the City and Eastward of St. Paul's

I

CROSBY Square on the east side of Bishopsgate Street reminds us of one of the residences of Sir John Crosby which occupied the site and a portion of which remained till recent years. The owner lived in the 15th century, and was Member of Parliament for the City, Sheriff and Mayor. There was a tradition that his name originated in his being born 'by a cross,' the cross indicated being that which gave a name to Cow-cross Street near Smithfield. As to this we may say with Stow, 'I holde it a fable.' The house was built:

of stone and timber verie large and beautifull

It was, or rather the site was,

letten to him by the Prioress of Saint Helens for ninetie neene yeares from 1466 for the annuall rent of eleven pound sixe shillings 8 pence.[1]

The owner enjoyed its occupation for a very brief time, as he died in 1475.

In Thomas Heywood's play of *Edward IV* he is made to say,[2]

> In Bishopsgate Street a poor house have I built
> And, as my name, have call'd it Crosby House
> And when as God shall take my life
> In little S. Helens I will be buried.

[1] Stow, *Survey* (1603), p. 174. The lease describes a house on the site
[2] 1600. I *Edward IV*, IV. ii.

A LITERARY TOPOGRAPHY OF OLD LONDON

Little St. Helen's was a house appertaining to the Priory of St. Helen's, and it is in the Church afterwards known as Great St. Helen's, that Sir John Crosby is buried, and where his monument may still be seen. He had been a considerable benefactor to the church.

Richard III, while Duke of Gloucester, seems to have occupied the house. Shakespeare has an allusion to this in a memorable scene. Richard, who has been addressing Anne with mock penitence and in the presence of the dead body of Henry VI, says,

> That it may please you leave these sad designes
> To him that hath most cause to be a mourner
> And presently repayre to Crosbie House [1]

In the next scene of the play he is giving directions to the murderers of his brother Clarence:

> When you have done, repayre to Crosby place,
> But sirs be sodaine in the execution
> Withall obdurate, do not heare him pleade
> For Clarence is well spoken and perhappes
> May moue your hearts to pitty [2]

Sir Thomas More was living at Crosby House in 1520, and it is possible that his 'Life of Richard III,' written about 1513, may have been composed in the very house occupied by Richard when Protector, and made the temporary residence of the boy-King Edward V. The house had many visitors:

> Little and little all folke . . . drew to Crosbies place in Bishopsgates strete where the protector kept his household. The protector had the resort, the King in maner dessolate.[3]

Shakespeare would probably know of this 'Life of Richard III' when he wrote his play. At a later period

---

[1] 1597. Shakespeare, *Richard III*, fol. 1623, I. ii.
[2] *Ibid.* I. iii.
[3] Sir Thos. More, *Works* (1557), p 53. Sir Thos More had a lease. Subsequently his daughter Margaret and her husband William Roper lived there. It was purchased by Sir John Spencer, Mayor in 1594. We also hear of Mary, Countess of Pembroke, Sidney's sister, living there. In 1674 a fire destroyed a great part of the mansion. See article in *Gentleman's Magazine*, 1836, part ii., Gomme, i. 44.

GRESHAM HOUSE

Sir Walter Raleigh lived there for a short time. At the beginning of the 17th century it was made use of for a magazine of arms and munitions. These were removed to the Tower, September 20, 1607.[1]

Judging from the Banqueting Hall, which remained till our own time, the house, which occupied a large site, must have been one of the most magnificent in the City. The Hall, late Gothic in character, had a richly carved timber roof, a lofty bay on one side and a minstrels' gallery at the end. During the 19th century it seems to have been neglected and fallen into disrepair. It was at one time occupied by a large wine merchant but, being renovated, served the purpose of dining-hall to a restaurant. There was danger of its utter destruction, as the value of the site had increased many hundred-fold since its founder paid the nuns of St. Helen's a rent of eleven pounds a year; but the public spirit of London was invoked, and the beautiful relic of 15th-century architecture was secured, and may now be seen re-erected on the Chelsea Embankment near to the site of the residence of Sir Thomas More, who for a time had been its occupant.

II

A century of time lay between the lives of Sir John Crosby and Sir Thomas Gresham, but they were both resident in the same parish and buried in the same Church of St. Helen's.

Sir Thomas Gresham's great wealth, high position in the City, and integrity of character earned for him favour with Queen Elizabeth, and in matters of finance she relied on his advice and benefited by his assistance. His wealth found many channels of usefulness. On the day of the opening of the Royal Exchange, his free gift to the City, the Queen visited him at his house in Bishopsgate Street opposite to that of Sir John Crosby

---
[1] *Summary of Parliaments*, No. 16.

and extending to Broad Street. This occupied a large site, the position indicated by the modern erection bearing his name.[1] The Queen was a frequent visitor, and it is of interest to quote from Sir Francis Walsingham's Journal if only to shew the rapidity of the Queen's movements—five visits in a ten-days' royal progress :

> May Anno 1576 Wednesday 9. Her Majestie went to Leycester Howse. Thursday 10 Her Majestie removid to Sir Thomas Greshams. Saturday 12 Her Majestie removid to my Lord Admirall's. Tewsday 15. Her Majesty removed to Nonesuch. Thursday 17. Her Majesty removid to Mr Caro's (Carey's) at Bedington Saturday 19 Her Majesty retourned to Greenwich.[2]

Sir Thomas by his will left his house in Bishopsgate Street to be a 'place for readings' as Stow phrases it, referring to the foundation of his College, which first found a home in his private residence.

Another citizen of some fame, Sir Paul Pindar, had a small but extremely beautiful residence in Bishopsgate Street, the street front of which was a most interesting specimen of old architecture, especially in the design of the upper windows. In later days it became a publichouse. The following excerpt from a tract of 1641 indicates Sir Paul's reputation for hospitality : [3]

> You are to be blam'd too, for not bidding farewell to Sir Paul Pinder (at whose beauteous house you have devoured the carcasse of many a cram'd Capon) before you fled.[4]

The front of this 'beauteous house' was carefully preserved when the building was taken down, and may be seen at South Kensington Museum.

In quite early times there were several large mansion-houses in Thames Street, having their principal frontage on the river. Baynard's Castle, the most conspicuous of these, has been already noticed, being at all events for

---

[1] The site in 1853 realised the large sum of over £136,000
[2] *Op cit*, 1570–83. *Camden Miscellanies*, vol. vi
[3] As to this see *London Churches before the Great Fire*, p. 99.
[4] *Four Fugitives Meeting*, tract on Sir John Suckling

COLD HARBOUR

a portion of its life a Royal Palace. Its name survives to this day, being the title of one of the City wards.

Sir John de Pulteney (or Poulteney), who died in 1349, was four times Lord Mayor. One of his many benefactions was to build the Church of All Hallows-the-Less. Adjoining the Church was the residence of the founder, acquired by him from a former owner (Sir John Abel is mentioned as the possessor in 1320). Stow writes:

> The Steeple and Quire of this Church standeth on an arched gate, being the entrie to a great house called 'Cold Harbrough.' [1]

Stow adds that the Quire fell down and was restored in his time (1594).

The house had many owners.

> In 1397 John Holland, Earl of Huntinton, was lodged there and Richard II his brother dined with him.

It appears to have been granted to Henry, Prince of Wales (afterwards Henry V), in 1410.[2]

There is another grant 'of the house called Coldearber' in 1483.[3]

In the reign of Henry VIII, when Durham House was taken by the Crown, the Bishop, Cuthbert Tunstal, had the use of 'Cold Harbrough,' and in the next reign we find the Earl of Shrewsbury there [4] and the place called 'Shrewsbury House.' In 1602 Gilbert Earl of Shrewsbury writes to Sir G. Carew, 'At my house in London this 27 Oct.'

An old plate shewed the house as it appeared in or about the year 1600. We see a Tudor building of five stories having five gables end-on to the river.[5] The

---

[1] *Survey* (1603), p. 237.
[2] See Rymer's *Fœdera* (Syllabus 565); also *Calendar of Patent Rolls*, Henry IV, p. 172. 'Grant for life to the King's son Henry Prince of Wales of an inn or place called "le Coldeherbergh."'
[3] *Ibid.* 716.
[4] On July 4, 1 Henry VIII, there was a grant for George, Earl of Shrewsbury, of the 'mansion called Cold Harborough ... in the King's hands by the death of the Countess of Richmond and Derby his grandmother having formerly belonged to the Duchy of Exeter.' See *Calendar of Letters and Papers Henry VIII*, vol. 1. p. 35.
[5] Produced in *London before the Fire*, B.M. 10350, i. 2.

A LITERARY TOPOGRAPHY OF OLD LONDON

derivation of Cold Harbrough (or Harbour) has given rise to many surmises, the name being known in over fifty places distant alike from sea or river. A cold situation is only a partial solution of the difficulty. In many cases the name simply implied a bare refuge for any comers—cold because no fire was provided.

Not far from the above, but to the north of Thames Street, on Dowgate Hill, was a house somewhat similar in name to the above, being called 'The Erber' (or Herbor). Stow writes of it:

> The great olde house called the Erber near to the Church of Saint Marie Bothaw. . . . Neuill Earle of Salisbury was lodged there 1457.

This was in the reign of Henry VI, during the wars. He brought with him 500 men. If they also were lodged, the house must have been large.

Stow continues:

> then it came to George, Duke of Clarence . . . by the gift of Edward the fourth . . It was lately new builded by Sir Thomas Pullison Maior and was afterwards inhabited by Sir Francis Drake that famous mariner.[1]

Thomas Starkey, about 1534, writes to 'Mayster Cromwell, Secretary to the Kynges Hyghnes,' and subscribes his letter

> Wryten at London in my lady of Salysburys place at Dowgate in such tyme as I was wrastlyng wyth my feuer.[2]

Starkey was Secretary to Lady Salisbury (Margaret Pole, daughter of the Duke of Clarence, and Countess in her own right). She was in disfavour with Henry VIII because as governess to the Princess Mary she refused on his marriage with Anne Boleyn to give up to the new queen the princess's jewels. Cardinal Pole was her son, a circumstance which added to the King's ill-feeling, as Pole had written a book adverse to the King's supremacy

---
[1] Stow, *Survey* (1603), p. 233.
[2] *Nine Historical Letters* (J. P. Collier, 1871).

COPPED HALL

over the Church.[1] The unfortunate lady was eventually included in an Act of Attainder and executed in 1541 under more than usually painful circumstances.

Near by in Dowgate stood a house known as 'Copped Hall.' In Thomas Rugge's 'Mercurius Politicus Redivivus,' June 1660, we read:

> His Maj^y [Charles II] at dinner at the Earl of Middlesex's house at Copt Hall.

This must have been Charles Sackville, first Earl of Middlesex. But according to Stow, writing in 1598, the house was in his time the Skinners' Hall, and had been so for many years.[2] There were, however, several houses of the same name, 'copped,' said to mean a pinnacle or, possibly, a pinnacle truncated or 'topped.' There was a 'Copped Hall' in the parish of St. Botolph Aldgate, and another in the parish of St. Andrew by the Wardrobe, and the existing 'Copthall Court' in Throgmorton Street indicates still one more. This is mentioned in 1662 in the account books of the Church of St. Bartholomew-by-the-Exchange.

Another house in the vicinity of Thames Street was appropriated to the Prince of Wales. This was at the corner of Crooked Lane and was described by Stow as 'a great House built of stone belonging to Edward the Black Prince,' but in his (Stow's) time converted into a hostelry. It was close to the 'Boar's Head' described by Shakespeare in *Henry IV*, and if Prince Henry lived in his predecessor's house we can understand the frequency of his visits to the Tavern.

Two other large mansion-houses dating from early times and also situated in Thames Street may be noted, the one the home of the Bygot family, the other that of the Scropes.

---

[1] *Pro Ecclesiasticae unitatis defensione.* See *Dict. of Nat. Biog.*
[2] Mr. Kingsford in his edition of Stow's *Survey* has a note of 'La Copped halle' in the parish of St. John Walbrook, the property of Roger de Dreyton in 1292. This appears to be the Dowgate House. There seems to have been a still earlier mention in 51 Henry III. (See Harben's *Dictionary of London*.)

A LITERARY TOPOGRAPHY OF OLD LONDON

Bygod (or Bygot) House was situate close to Broken Wharf, and occupied a large site facing the river. Stow describes it as

> One large olde building of stone with arched gates ... in the reign of Henry the third the 43 yeare pertaining unto Hugh de Bygot.[1]

In the 'Calendar of Charter Rolls,' 11 Edward II,[2] we find on May 12, 1318:

> Gift to Thomas Earl of Norfolk, Marshall of England, the King's brother, houses at Broken Wharf late Roger le Bygod.

Between Baynard Castle and Paul's Wharf was a large mansion built round an inner courtyard and having a frontage to the river. This was the residence of the Scrope family. Stow says, 'belonging to them, in the 31 of Henry 6'; but he describes 'Burley House' as being in the same position as 'a great messuage ... comming to the hands of Edward the 3 and being given to Sir Simon Burley.' It would appear that the Burley family first owned the house and that the Scropes were their successors at a later period.[3] Sir Simon Burley served in France with the Black Prince, but in the next reign (Richard II) he was attainted with other favourites of the King and beheaded.

There was also a Scrope Inn in Holborn close to St. Andrew's Church. Richard le Scrope, first Baron Scrope of Bolton, who died in 1403, was the owner. He was a lawyer, and possibly for that reason let the house for a time to one of the Societies of Serjeants-at-law, and for a certain period it was known as one of the lesser Inns of Court or Chancery.

There was a smaller residence in Thames Street close to Paul's Wharf belonging to the Earls of Huntingdon, descendants of William Hastings, Lord Chamberlain to

---

[1] *Survey* (1603), p. 364.
[2] Vol. 1 p. 376
[3] Stow's *Survey* (1603), p 366.

DERBY HOUSE

Edward IV, who gave it to him, it having in earlier times been in the possession of the Bewmount family in the reign of Edward III.

In the same locality as the houses just described, though not facing the river, was Derby House, the home of the Stanleys. The house was on Paul's Wharf Hill and originally built by Thomas Stanley, the first Earl. In the reign of Edward VI it was exchanged for land at Knowsley and thus came to the Crown. Queen Mary gave it to the Heralds' College, but the title of Derby House was continued for many years. There are many allusions to it, especially in political tracts and poems, as it was used for important Parliamentary Committees, especially at the period just before King Charles's execution and during the Interregnum. The titles of several tracts, all dated 1648, shew how impassioned was party feeling at the time.

Westminster Proiects, or the mysterie of Darby House discovered, being an Anatomy of the designs of the present Grandees of Parliament and Army acting as Councel of State and Darby House.[1]

'The Divell of Derby House' was another:

> Those sonnes of sin at Derby House that sit
> Who out-strip Machiavel in damned wit
> Have put this treaty on with an intent
> To ruin Charles and kingly government.[2]

The writer calls the Committee 'The Black Conclave of Conspirators sitting at Derby House.' Another Tract of 1648 gives:

further discovery of the mystery of the Committee of Grandees at Darby House.

> They juggle still on all hands and like knaves
> Project all wayes to make the people slaves.

The Committee or some of them are named. Amongst others 'Vane junior, Haselrig, Crumwel, Manchester, etc.' Three years before the Restoration we get the lament of a Royalist in Bishop Henry King's Elegy on Sir C. Lucas

[1] Forster Collection, No. 1596.   [2] Forster Collection.

A LITERARY TOPOGRAPHY OF OLD LONDON

and Sir George Lisle (Royalists who defended Colchester and on the surrender of the town were shot—murdered, King says) :

> We all your Juggles both for Time and Place
> From Darby House to Westminster can trace,
> The Circle where the factious Jangles meet
> To trample Law and Gospel under feet [1]

After the Restoration we find an allusion in a poem by Andrew Marvell, one of Cromwell's old adherents. It would appear that Derby House was always in disfavour whatever party was in power:

> These must assist her in her countermines
> To overthrow the Derby House designs [2]

On December 9, 1558, Sir Nicholas Bacon writes to Dr. Parker :

> I would wish that you should repair to London with as convenient speed as you can, where you shall find me at Burgeny house in Paternoster Row [3]

This was the London residence of the Earls of Abergavenny and was, according to Stow, 'one great house built of stone and timber at the north end of Ave Mary Lane.' In the reigns of Edward II and III it was the residence of John, Duke of Bretagny and Earl of Richmond, and in the reign of Richard II of the Earl of Pembroke. The house is the one that afterwards became the Stationers' Hall and was destroyed in the Fire.[4]

At that period of its history when the Charterhouse had ceased to be a Monastery and before it became a hospital and school, it was occupied as a private house and known by the name of its owner or occupier for the time being. In Cecil's Journal, July 1, 1571, there is the following reference to it:

> The Duke of Norfolk was prisoner in his own house, called Howard House.[5]

---

[1] 1657.
[2] 1667. *Instructions to a Painter*.
[3] *Parker Correspondence* (Parker Society), Part III. 49.
[4] See *Gentleman's Magazine*, 1820, Pt. I
[5] Quoted in Strype's *Annals*, B. I c. 9

NEWCASTLE HOUSE

Shortly after the Duke was committed to the Tower for alleged complicity with Mary Queen of Scots. Stow does not mention Howard House by name, but in referring to 'the late dissolued Monasterie' he adds that the Duke of Norfolk has 'made large and sumptuous buildinges both for lodging and pleasure.'

Not far off was the house of the Duke of Newcastle (William Cavendish). It was in Clerkenwell Close, on the site of St. Mary's Priory, and some portions of it remained till 1826.[1] The Duke was a strong supporter of the King in the Civil War and his estates were confiscated. The Duchess Margaret wrote her husband's life, and made vigorous efforts to get back the family estates. The following from Evelyn's 'Diary' shews that they were in Clerkenwell in 1667. The Duke and Duchess were both writers of poetry and drama, but their works are but little known.

> I went to make court to the Duke and Duchess of Newcastle at their house in Clerkenwell being newly come out of the North. . . I was much pleased with the extraordinary fanciful habit, garb and discourse of the Duchess.[2]

The opinion of Samuel Pepys as a literary critic does not carry much weight :

> Staid at home reading the ridiculous History of my Lord Newcastle wrote by his wife ; which shows her to be a mad, conceited, ridiculous woman, and he an asse to suffer her to write.[3]

The Earl of Southampton's house in Holborn has already been alluded to. There was, according to Stow, another house belonging to the family and called 'Garter House,' from the owner's official position :

> Adjoyning to (the Barbican) is one other great-house called Garter House some time builded by Sir Thomas Writhesley . . . Garter principall King of Armes . . . in the top thereof a Chappell which he dedicated by the name of 'S. Trinitatis in alto.'[4]

---

[1] The Nuns' Hall being used as a workshop (see Pink's *History of Clerkenwell*).
[2] Evelyn, *Diary*, April 18, 1667.
[3] *Diary*, March 18, 1667-8.
[4] *Survey* (1603), p. 304

A LITERARY TOPOGRAPHY OF OLD LONDON

But it should be noted that the father of the above Sir Thomas, viz. Sir John Wriothesley, who died in 1504, was also Garter King-at-Arms and head of the College of Heralds.[1] Near the foregoing, also in Barbican, was what appears to be the earliest house of the Suffolk family, built by Robert de Ufford, the first Earl, who fought at Crecy. The 'plot or seate' of this, so Stow says, 'King Edward III in 1336 gaue unto Robert Ufford Earle of Suffolke by the name of his Mannor of Base-court.' This is evidently the house alluded to in a little-known play by Thomas Drue entitled ' The Dutches of Suffolke.'

> With some especiall servants of the Queene
> Enter the Dutches house in Barbican
> Take a true Inventory of all her goods
> Discharge her household save a man or two
> And say you have commandment from the Queene.[2]

It was said that there was yet another Suffolk House near the Tower and built on the site of the suppressed Convent of Minorites, and occupied by the Duke of Suffolk who was executed in Queen Mary's reign (Henry Grey, father of Lady Jane Grey). There is a tradition that his head was mummified and preserved in the Chapel of the suppressed Convent or the Church of the Holy Trinity built there at a later date.[3]

At the dissolution of the Priory of the Holy Trinity, Henry VIII gave the house to Sir Thomas Audley in recognition of his services in the dispute with Wolsey and the matter of the divorce of Queen Katherine. Sir Thomas Audley, who was Lord Chancellor in 1533, converted the buildings into a private house, which in time became the property of his only daughter, who married the Duke of Norfolk and predeceased him. The Duke thus became the owner. Hence the name 'Duke's Place,' which still survives. The house had several subsequent owners, and was still standing, though in a ruinous condition through a fire, at the beginning of the last century. An old plate

---

[1] See *Dict. of Nat. Biog.*
[2] *Op. cit.* 1631, I 1
[3] See *The Tower of London*, Rich. Davey (1910), p 207.

ROSE MANOR

shews portions of the ancient Priory as well as the later additions.[1]

Sir Nicholas Bacon, Lord Keeper, built a house in Noble Street at the north-west corner of Oat Lane, which bore his name. Stow says the site was previously occupied by a much older house, the home of the Shelley family, and he mentions Sir Thomas Shelley as owner in 1 Henry IV.[2] In after years the Scriveners' Company had their Hall there.

Behind where the Mansion House now stands was an ancient house, the property of the Pollexfen family. It was burnt down in the Great Fire, but Sir Henry Pollexfen, barrister, who prosecuted the followers of Monmouth and defended the Seven Bishops, and who was afterwards Chief Justice of the Common Pleas, rebuilt it. There is still a house bearing the name.

Edward Stafford, the third Duke of Buckingham, also known as Edward Bohun, had a house in Suffolk Lane,[3] Candlewick Street, called 'Rose Manor.' This was the Duke, one of Wolsey's victims, who with the aid of suborned evidence was attainted for high treason and executed in 1521. The story is told in Shakespeare's *Henry VIII*, and the house is alluded to by one of the witnesses at the trial.

> The Duke being at the Rose within the Parish S. Lawrence Poultney, did of me demand What was the speech among the Londoners concerning the French journey.[4]

One of the customs of the Manor seems to have given rise to the title, viz. the granting of leases at a nominal rent consisting of the payment of a rose once a year. An Indenture of the Bishop dated at the Manor of Rose 21 April,

---

[1] See *European Magazine*, Sept. 1802, and Lambert's *History of London* (1808), ii. 391.
[2] Stow, *Survey* (1603), p. 306. The *Dict. of Nat. Biog.* does not give this Sir Thomas, but mentions a Sir Richard Shelley (temp. Henry VIII), last Grand Prior of the Knights of St John.
[3] Suffolk Lane, originally so named from the Suffolk family. William de la Pole, Duke of Suffolk, was living there about 1446 (See note in Mr. Kingsford's edition of Stow's *Survey*, vol. ii. p 322.)
[4] *Henry VIII*, I. ii.

1403, in respect to a small piece of land, part of the Bishop's Inn without the new Temple Bar, leased for building houses for a term of thirty years, the rent for the first ten years being the payment of a rose at midsummer and for the remaining years 6s. 8d. per annum. In after times the house in Suffolk Lane became the Merchant Taylors' School.

There was another 'Buckingham House' occupied by John Sheffield, Duke of Buckingham. This was 'Goring House' (q.v.). The present Buckingham Palace is on the site.

Not far from the above, and standing in St. Swithin's Lane on the north side of the Church, was 'Oxford Place,' the home of the ancient family of the de Veres. Stow, writing at the end of Queen Elizabeth's reign, says:

> The late Earle of Oxford hath beene noted within these fortie yeares to have ridden into this Citie and so to his house by London Stone with 80 gentlemen in a liuery of Reading Tawny and Chains of gold about their necks and a hundred yeomen in the like liuery . . . all hauing his cognizance of the blew Bore.[1]

The house was formerly pertaining to the Prior of Tortington, in Sussex. The present Oxford Court, Cannon Street, marks the vicinity. In 1566 Queen Elizabeth went there to meet the Earl of Leicester. So Stow writes in the 'Historical Memoranda' which he left in MS. and which have been printed by the Camden Society. Why the Queen should go there to meet her favourite Dudley does not appear, seeing that he had a house on the river, which afterwards became Essex House.

> The 2 of Aprell yᵉ Erle of Leycester cam to London Stone to yᵉ Erle of Oxfords place in S Swythyns Church Yarde where it was apoyntyd that the Quenes Majestie . . . to mett with the sayd Earle.

The Earl came in great state with a retinue of 700 followers, but the Queen came from Greenwich very privately:

> taking a whiry with one payr of ors for her and two othar ladyes at S. Mary Overys stayres and so rowed over to the Three Cranes . . . and so to the sayd Oxford Place.

---

[1] *Survey* (1603), pp. 89–90.

THOMAS CROMWELL'S HOUSE

but either through mistake or for some untold reason, the Earl left before the Queen's arrival and did not see his Royal Mistress until on the return journey he waited for her near St. George's Church.

> She cam owt of her Coche in the highe way and she imbrased ye earle and kyssed hym thrise and then they rode togyther to Grenewytche.[1]

In the reign of Henry V the de Vere family owned a mansion-house situate in the parish of St. Augustine-in-the-Wall and lying between St. Mary Axe and Bishopsgate Street. In Stow's time this was in a ruined condition

A house contiguous to the above is mentioned in the 'State Papers,' Henry VIII, as being the residence of Edmund Dudley, Speaker of the House of Commons, 1504, and executed for alleged high treason in 1510, it having been stated that he had recommended his friends to arm themselves in the event of the death of Henry VII. An inventory of the plate, jewellery and other valuables in his house was made in 1509 and incidentally indicates that the mansion was one of some distinction. The various apartments are mentioned, such as 'the long gallery next the garden,' the 'square chamber,' with many other 'galleries, parlours' etc.[2] The adjoining house, occupied by Sir Richard Empson, Chancellor of the Duchy of Lancaster, had also a garden, and both of them had 'a doore of entercourse' (so Stow says) to the garden of Oxford Place.

Thomas Lord Cromwell, when his career was at its zenith, built himself a mansion in Throgmorton Street, adjacent to the Monastery of the Augustine Friars. The site not being quite sufficient for his needs, he annexed without leave or permission a portion of his neighbours' land Stow tells the story, his own father being one of the sufferers. A summer-house or some such erection

---

[1] Camden Society (1880), p. 137.
[2] *Cal. of State Papers Henry VIII* (1509), *Domestic*, p 425.

being 'lowsed from the ground' and moved 'upon rollers 22 foot.' Stow moralises:

> The suddaine rising of some men causeth them to forget themselves . . . My father paid his whole rent which was vjs. viijd. the yeare for that halfe which was left.[1]

Cromwell was living there, or at all events in possession, in 1523, for in that year he writes:

> To my beloved wyf Elyzabeth Cromwell agenst the Freyers Augustines in London be this given.

Thirteen years after he writes:

> At my howse at the Rolles.

He was Master of the Rolls in 1534, and had an official residence in Chancery Lane.

The Earls of Sussex had a house in Bermondsey built on the site of the old Abbey (Abbey Street still records the locality), 'a goodly house builded of stone and timber'—so Stow describes it. The following is worth quoting, though this is not a work on field-botany, because it is taken from Gerard's 'Herbal,' a work of some fame, and also because lovers of wild flowers will like to know that the familiar flower spoken of grew in the 16th century, as it does to this day, in the vicinity of houses in London, though it would not be found in Bermondsey as we now know it.

> The other sort [that is of *Solanum*] with white flowers, I found in a ditch side against the garden wall of the Right honorable the Earle of Sussex, his house in Bermondsey Streete.[2]

One more house on the Surrey side may be mentioned. Out of the ruins of the Priory of St. Mary Overie Sir Anthony Browne built a residence afterwards known as Montague House, from his son Anthony, first Viscount Montague. The latter, though a Roman Catholic, was loyal to Edward VI and Queen Elizabeth, whom he entertained at Cowdray in Sussex at the well-known house built by his father, the

---

[1] *Survey* (1603), p 181.
[2] *Catalogus Arborum . . . in horto Johannis Gerardi*, 1596 (Wood Night-shade, *Solanum Dulcamara*). See note in *Herbal* (1597).

MONTAGUE HOUSE

ruins of which only now remain. The following quotation from Walter Yonge's Diary [1] appears to refer to this Montague House, though the first Viscount died in 1592.

> About this time there came into England eight Jesuits, or seminaries, from France whereof three were taken in the Lord Montague his house in Southwark [2]

Montague House, Bloomsbury, belongs to a later period, and was built by the first Duke of Montague ' on a French plan,' so Pennant says The Duke had been Ambassador in France It was in this house that the British Museum was first started.

A reference to Bloomsbury reminds us that there was anciently a house known as Bloomsbury House, which probably gave a name to the district. In the reign of Edward II ' Richard de Gloucester held a messuage called Bloemundesbury, in the Parish of S. Giles of the lepers.' At his death the King learns by an Inquisition that ' Richard held the aforesaid messuage and land in chief by the service of rendering a sore-coloured sparrowhawk to the Exchequer at the Gule of August.' [3]

Another house in Southwark has historic interest. This was the house of Lord Monteagle and was situate close to St. Mary Overie Church and Winchester House. It was to this house that the letter disclosing the Gunpowder Plot was sent It was still standing, in a somewhat ruinous condition, at the beginning of the 19th century [4]

Stow has no mention of any residence of a citizen of such prominence as Sir Richard Whittington, thrice Lord Mayor, the use of his great wealth being best remembered by the munificence of his foundations. But it is recorded that he had a house known as Whittington's Palace in Hart Street near Mark Lane, and an old engraving shews a building of some dignity and pretension having richly carved timber work and occupying three sides of a square.

---

[1] *Op cit* 1606 (Camden Society), p 7
[2] See *Dict. of Nat Biog.*
[3] *Calendar of Close Rolls*, Aug 20, 1324.
[4] See *Gentleman's Magazine*, 1808, part ii. p. 777.

A LITERARY TOPOGRAPHY OF OLD LONDON

It was still standing in 1796, though in a dilapidated condition.[1]

As already mentioned with other Bishops' Palaces, Suffolk Place, Southwark, was given by Queen Mary to the Archbishop of York, but used by him for a short time only. Its foundation dated from the time of Henry VIII, being built by Charles Brandon for the Duke of Suffolk. Stow called it a 'large and most sumptuous house, over against St. George's Church . . coming after into the Kinge's hands . . . was called Southwarke Place.' Stow adds 'a mint of coynage was there kept for the King.'[2] But we find it still called Suffolk Place in the reign of Edward VI and Queen Mary. Sir John Hayward, in his 'Life of Edward VI,' says :

> The Marshall and other French Commissioners were saluted . . with all the shot of more than fifty of the King's great ships . and lastly were lodged in Suffolk Palace in Southwark . . . they had more than 400 gentlemen in their train[3]

The following extract shews that Princess Elizabeth was lodged there :

> Account of Robert Kyrton master of the barge for serving of the Queen's grace from Chelsey to Barnette's Castyll . . . similarly my lady Elizabeth from Suffolk Place to Chelsea. Total 3l. 12s.

In recording the reception of King Philip, Dr. Heylin writes

> From thence the Court removed to Richmond by land and so by water to Suffolk Place in the Borough of Southwark[4]

Fabyan in his 'Chronicle' describes the Royal progress of Philip and Mary (1554).

> Also the xviij daie of August the Kyng and the quene came to Suffolke Place in Southwarke and there dined and after diner with most part of the nobilitie of the realme roade right royally ouer Londō Bridge.[5]

---

[1] See Lambert's *Hist of London*, 1808, vol. ii. pp 388–9, also *Gentleman's Magazine*, 1796, part ii. 545.
[2] Stow's *Survey* (1603), p. 413
[3] *Op cit* 1636, p 303
[4] *Ecclesia Restaurata*, 1661 (1849, ii. 130).
[5] 1559. *Continuation of Fabyan's Chronicle*

CHAPTER V
The Parliament Houses and Courts of Justice

CHAPTER V

The Parliament Houses and Courts of Justice

I

THE ancient Palace of the Kings of England at Westminster occupied the site or a portion of the site of the present Houses of Parliament, and has already been described in a former chapter. In the Great Hall which was its leading feature and is all that is left to us of its primal grandeur, the Kings held their Parliament and administered justice.

As time went on many additional buildings were erected in contiguity to the Palace, but with 16th and 17th century writers the term Palace of Westminster may be found to mean any part or whole collectively. In time we hear of the 'Parliament House' and the Houses of Lords and Commons as separate buildings, and the like with the Star Chamber and other apartments or buildings devoted to a particular purpose . also of the various Courts of Law by name.

The position of the Hall was not sufficiently high to preserve it from occasional floods, the River not being embanked.

> In the yeare 1230 the riuer of Thames overflowing the bankes in the great Palace of Westminster men did row with wheryes in the middle of the Hall.[1]

And in 1578:

> The Thames did rise so highe, after the dissolution of the snow, that Westminster Hall was drowned and much fishe lefte there in the pallace yard when the water returned [2]

[1] Stow, *Survey* (1603), p. 468
[2] W. Harrison, MS. *Chronology* (Furnivall).

A LITERARY TOPOGRAPHY OF OLD LONDON

Nor did it escape danger by fire, although it was spared in 1512 when a great part of the Palace was destroyed, for in Archbishop Laud's Diary we read:

> Feb. 20, 1630 —This Sunday morning Westminster Hall was found on fire by the burning of the little shops or stalls kept there It was taken in time

Stow has little to say of Parliament, except as held in the Great Hall, but he mentions a temporary building put up in 1397 by Richard II when the Hall was out of repair:

> Richard . . . hauing occasion to hold a Parliament caused for that purpose a large house to be builded in the middest of the Palace Court . . . very large and being made of tymber and couered with tyle open on both sides and at both the endes that all men might see and heare [1]

As to the House in his time James Howell writes.

> Having visited God Almighties House, we will now take a view of the chief Prætorium of Great Britain which is Westminster Hall, and of the Courts of Judicature which are thereunto annexed, and first of the Court Paramount, the high national Court of Parliament,[2] which great Councel was used to be the bulwark of our liberties, the boundary and bank which kept us from slavery, from the inundations of tyrannical encroachments and unbounded evill-Government [3]

Only two years after the work of repair above mentioned, Richard having in the Tower renounced his title to the throne :

> This renunciation was openly red in Westminster Halle; and every State singulerly inqwyred how thei likid this. And thei saide alle thei consented theretoo [4]

As a Court of Justice the Hall was used only on state occasions or some case of supreme importance, such as the

---

[1] *Survey* (1603), p. 471
[2] 'The High Court of Parliament' is the apt phrase used in the Prayer Book.
[3] 1657. *Londinopolis*, p 356.
[4] Capgrave's *Chronicle*, Rolls, 272

WESTMINSTER HALL

trial of King Charles I, as described by a contemporary biographer:

> Having proclaimed their wicked purposes and dress'd up a tribunal at the upper end of Westminster Hall with all the shapes of terror, where the President with his abject and bloody assistants were placed, thither afterwards they bring this most excellent monarch . . . the people . . . crouding in (the great gates of the Hall being flung open) did bewail in him the frailty of our Humane condition.[1]

The Hall is frequently referred to by writers in connexion with law and law cases and with lawyers and their ways; but the term 'Westminster Hall' is used to indicate the various Courts which in course of time surrounded the Great Hall. The following extract from Sir Thomas Smyth's 'De Republica Anglorum' shews that in early times the several Courts of Law were held in the Great Hall itself:

> In times past . . . the courtes and benches followed the King and his Court wheresoeuer he went, especially shortly after the Conquest. Which thing being found very cumbersome, paineful and chargeable to the people, it was agreed by Parliament that there should be a standing place where judgements should be giuen and it hath long time been in Westminster Hall which King William Rufus builded for the hall of his own house. In that hall be ordinarily seene Tribunals or Judges seats At the entry on the right hand the commonplace where civil matters are to be pleaded especially such as touch lands or contractes At the upper end of the Hall on the right hand the Kinges bench where pleas of the Crown have their place and on the left hand sitteth the Chancellor accompanyed by the Master of the Roules (*custos Archiuorum regis*) and certaine men learned in the civill lawe called Masters of the Chauncerie (*assessores*)[2]

The following quotation from Norden points to the terrors of the law and the profits of the lawyer:

> Westminster Hall is known to manie, a terror to a multitude and a golden myne to some.[3]

---

[1] R. Royston, 1662, *Life and Works of Charles I*.
[2] 1583, p. 53.
[3] 1592. J. Norden (*Harl. MS*).

A LITERARY TOPOGRAPHY OF OLD LONDON

And in the same vein, though from a much earlier writer:

> But nowe a dayes he shall haue his intent
> That hath most gold and so it is befall
> That aungels worke wonders in Westminster hall.[1]

In Term time the Hall would doubtless be thronged. Many went from curiosity, as Barnabee Rych writes:

> Shall we yet make a stepp to Westminster Hall, a little to ouerlook the lawyers.[2]

Nash's satire on the lawyers was, as most satires of the time were, much overdone.

> If in one man a whole legion of diuells have been billetted how manie hundred thousand legions repair to a tearme at London. . . . In Westminster Hall a man can scarce breath for them.[3]

'The Painted Chamber,' often alluded to, was a comparatively small apartment used for special purposes. An old plan in Smith's 'Antiquities of London' shews this chamber adjoining the House of Lords on one side and the Court of Requests on the other. It was here that the last scene in the trial of Charles I took place.

> The Court adjourned into the Painted Chamber, and upon serious consideration declared the King to be a tyrant, traitor, murderer, and a publick enemy to the Commonwealth: that his condemnation extend unto death, by severing his head from his body, and that a sentence grounded upon those votes be prepared.[4]

II

Parliaments are mentioned before the reign of Edward I, but the first complete and regularly constituted Parliament of the Three Estates, viz. the Clergy, the Nobility and the Commonalty, was in 1275.

---

[1] Barclay, *Shyp of Folys*, fol. 4 (1508).
[2] Barnabee Rych, *Honestie of this Age* (1614).
[3] 1590. *Terrors of the Night*, B 4.
[4] 1649. *Memoirs of General Ludlow* (1894), i. 216. Ludlow was one of those who signed the death warrant.

PARLIAMENT HOUSES

Of earlier Parliaments William Prynne writes:

> At least till 49 Henry III our English Parliaments were only of the King, Lords spiritual and temporal and Peers and Barons of the Realm.[1]

It is clear that the Parliament met in places other than Westminster Hall, e.g. in Hall's 'Chronicle' (Anno 14 Henry VIII) we read, 'The xv day of April began a Parliament at the Blacke Fryers and that day the Masse of the holy ghost was sung.'[2] But long before this the Chapter House of the Abbey was in use.

> I find of Record the 50 of Ed. the 3 that the Chapter House of the Abbot of Westminster was then the usual house for the Commons in Parliament.[3]

Pennant says that they sat there till 1547, when Edward VI granted the Chapel of St. Stephen to their use.

The term in general use was 'The Parliament House,' indicating the place of assembly of both Lords and Commons. An engraving by Hollar (1641) shews this a detached building a little to the west of Westminster Hall, Gothic in design, with pinnacled buttresses and, apparently, a flat roof. A rare tract, printed at Nuremberg in 1542 and entitled 'The Lamentacyon of a Christen agaynst the Cytye of London,' alludes to the Parliament with contemptuous disrespect:

> O ye deuelles, ye blynde guydes and seducers of the people, haue of late bewytched you the Parliament House . . . caused actes and decrees to be made so cleane contrarye to the lawes of the lyvinge God.[4]

In the time of Elizabeth a visitor describes the inside of the House, and relates a tradition which had been imposed upon his credulity.

In the Chamber where the Parliament is usually held, the seats

---

[1] *Hist. Collect. of the Ancient Parliaments of England* (1649), p 316.
[2] *Op. cit.* 1548 (1809, p 652).
[3] *Survey* (1603), p 471.
[4] *Roderigo Mors* (Henry Brinkelow), c vj.

141

and wainscot are made of wood, the growth of Ireland, said to have that occult quality that all poisonous animals are driven away by it.[1]

The following relates to the powder conspiracy in the next reign:

> Thomas Percy hired an house at Westminster for that purpose neere adjoyning to the Parliament House and there we begun to make our myne about the 11 of December 1604 [2]

When Guy Fawkes was arrested, he was, after the barbarous custom of the day, put to the torture to enforce a confession. The following holograph letter of the King may be seen in the Museum of the Public Record Office:

> 6 Novr 1605. If he will not otherwayes confesse the gentler tortours are to be first used unto him *et sic per gradus ad ima tenditur* and so God speed youre goode worke. James R.

A little later we find the House of Commons mentioned by name. Bacon speaks of Mr. (afterwards Lord Chief Justice) Popham as 'Speaker of the House of Commons,' and tells this story:

> When he was Speaker and the House of Commons had sate long and done in effect nothing, coming one day to Q. Elizabeth, she said to him, 'Now Mr. Speaker what hath passed in the Commons House?' He answered, 'If it please your Majesty, seven weeks.' [3]

In Stuart times the ceremony of opening Parliament in State was in full force, and King Charles I went in procession, sometimes by water.

> The King's Majesty in his Parliamentary Robes and Crowne, his Majesty's train borne by three Earles or Lord's eldest sonnes, preceded by the Heralds the Lord Privy Seal . . . the Archbishop of Canterbury etc. . . The King on horseback as far as Westminster. Then on foot to the Parliament House [4]

In 1643 Archbishop Laud enters in his Diary:

> May 23. This day the Queen (i.e. Henrietta Maria) was voted a traytor in the Commons House.

[1] 1598. Hentzner, *Travels*, tr.
[2] 'Declaration of Guido Fawkes,' *Works James I* (1616), p. 232
[3] Bacon, *Apophthegms*.
[4] *Manners of London Parliaments*, W. Hakewill, 1641,

HOUSE OF LORDS

This was Laud's last entry in his Diary, which was forcibly taken from him in the Tower and used in evidence against him at his trial.

The term 'House of Lords' is but rarely used. In 'Fragmenta Regalia' it is called 'the higher house.' The following is from the 'Memoirs of Edmund Ludlow' already cited. He is describing a riot shortly before the King's execution:

> Some of them (the mob) getting to the windows of the House of Lords, threw stones in upon them and threatened them with worse usage [1]

During the Protectorate the House of Lords was abolished by the Commons. This was the ordinance passed in 1648.

> The Commons of England assembled in Parliament, finding by too long experience that the house of Lords is useless and dangerous have thought fit to ordain and enact that from henceforth the house of Lords in Parliament shall be and is hereby wholly abolished . . . and that the Lords shall not from henceforth meet and sit in the said house called the Lords House [2]

In a news-letter, Jan. 23, 1657, we read of Cromwell:

> His Highness came by water to the House formerly called The Lords' House where a Canopy and Chair of State was prepared for him [3]

The House met on the very day of the execution of the King. This is an extract from the Journal. No mention whatever is made of the King:

> Die Martis 30° die Januarii
> Prayers by Mr Salwey.

Five Lords were present, including the Speaker There was some trifling business and a petition from a Fellow of St. John's College, Cambridge

But two days afterwards, on February 1, 1648–9, six

---

[1] 1647, July 26
[2] Collection of H. Scoble, Clerk of the Parliament.
[3] *Clarke Papers*, III p 122

peers, including the Speaker Denbigh, being present, the entry in the Journal is:

> Die Jovis 1º die Februarii.
> Prayers by Mr. Rayner.
> It being moved · That the House would take into consideration the settlement of the Government of England and Ireland in this present conjunction of things upon the death of the King.

In Baker's 'Chronicle' concerning the year 1659, one year before the Restoration, we read 'The Upper House, as it now began to be called.'[1] Laud used that term

During the Civil War a curious scene might have been witnessed at Westminster, when in the presence of the Lords and Commons, August 11, 1646, the Great Seal was destroyed Depicted in 'A sight of the transactions of these latter yeares.'[2] The plate, said to be by Hollar, shews a man with a sledge hammer smashing the Seal.

III

The Star Chamber, so named, because, we are told,

> at the first all the roofe thereof was decked with images of starres gilted,[3]

is very frequently referred to, partly because, whether rightly or wrongly, it was very unpopular Yet Sir John Harington in one of his epigrams gives it an honourable reputation :

> The Court that Corne from Cockle sifts,
> Star Chamber that of Justice is the mirror.[4]

William Lambarde speaks of it as the 'Councill Chamber of that Pallace (Westminster) that hath obtained that dignity to bear a name above others,' and he alludes

---
[1] *Baker's Chron continued*, p 697
[2] J Vicars, 1642.
[3] a. 1577 Sir T. Smith, *Commonwealth of England*, III iv
[4] Epig. 48 (1615).

STAR CHAMBER

to Henry VI and VII, who ' did personally sit in judgement ' there.[1] He suggests another derivation of the word, viz.:

> From the English word Steoran which signifieth to steare or rule as doth the Pilot of a Ship because the King and Councell doe sit here as it were at the sterne and doe governe the shippe of the Common-wealth.[2]

Bacon in his ' Life of Henry VII ' speaks with respect and appreciation of the high functions of the Court:

> This Court is one of the sagest and noblest institutions of this Kingdom . . . and as the Chancery had the pretorian power for equity, so the Star Chamber had the censorian power for offences under the degree of capital. This Court is compounded of good elements for it consisteth of four kinds of persons—counsellors, peers, prelates, and chief judges. It discerneth also principally of four kinds of causes—forces, frauds, crimes various of stellionate,[3] and the inchoations or middle acts towards crimes capital or heinous, not actually committed or perpetrated.

Corruption, bribery or the threatening of a juryman, for which the term cozenage was used, were offences punishable by the Court. In an old play we read:

> I will Star Chamber you all for cozenage.[4]

A writer, referring to the time of Charles I, speaks of the Chamber as being the

> Scourge and torture of the Commonwealth by imprisonments and mutilation.[5]

The Court certainly used torture, the legality of which was doubtful. Punishment for slander was very severe. In 1630 (according to Baker's ' Chronicle '):

> Dr. Leighton was sentenced in the Star Chamber to have his body whipt, his forehead stigmatiz'd, his ears cropt and his nose slit for exhorting the late Parliament to smite the Bishops under the sixth rib and for calling the Queen the daughter of Heth . . . in his book called Sions Plea.

[1] 1591. *Archeion* (1635), pp. 165, 176, 178.
[2] *Archeion*, p. 155.
[3] Crafty, like a lizard.
[4] *Ram Alley*, by Barry.
[5] Sir A. Weldon, *Court of K. Charles I* (1651), p. 203.

A LITERARY TOPOGRAPHY OF OLD LONDON

Prynne was 'censured' there, as the term was, for his book 'Histriomastix,' an attack on plays with some scandal as to the Queen's encouragement of Masques. Prynne was a much hated man, and Ben Jonson's allusion to his punishment in a play is not to be wondered at.

> One that hath lost his ears by a just sentence
> In the Star-Chamber, a right valiant knave [1]

In *The Merry Wives of Windsor* Shallow threatens to indict Sir John Falstaff:

> Sir Hugh, perswade me not. I will make a Star-Chamber matter of it. If hee were twenty Sir John Falstaffs he shall not abuse Robert Shallow Esquire.

In 1590 the Clerkship of the Star Chamber was granted by patent to Francis Bacon, and a memorandum to that effect was in the Note Book of Lord Burleigh. But possession was deferred [2]

It is worth remembering that a 'Decree of Star Chamber concerning printing,' made July 11, 1637, was the cause of Milton's speech afterwards printed as 'Areopagitica.' Also that by a decree of the same Chamber a copy of every new book printed was to be deposited at Stationers' Hall, to be sent to Bodley's Library, Oxford.

IV

The general reputation of the Courts as a means of obtaining justice does not seem to have been very high. In one of his epigrams, Sir John Davies says:

> Westminster is a mill that grinds all causes but grind his cause for mee there he yᵗ list

As to the Court of King's Bench, in a supposed dialogue

---

[1] 1640. *Magnetic Lady*, III. iv.
[2] See Spedding's *Life of Bacon*.

COURT OF KING'S BENCH

between Cardinal Pole and Lupset, the former says, referring to a plaintiff:

> Yf he be purposyd to vex hys aduersary, he wyl by wryte remoue hys cause to the Court at Westmynstur; by the wych mean oft tymys the unjust cause preuaylyth.[1]

The following points to the easiness of obtaining false evidence:

> Why, I have been a post-knight in Westminster this twelve years and sworn to that which no one else would venture on.[2]

'The Royallest Court in the Land' is James Howell's expression:

> In this Court the Kings have sat as being the highest Bench and the Judges of that Court on the lower Bench at his feet; but Judicature only belongeth to the Judges of that Court and in his presence they answer all motions.[3]

Shakespeare, in *Henry IV*, tells how Prince Hal flouted the Lord Chief Justice in this Court, *sc.* in King's Bench. The story is well told by Sir Thomas Elyot in 'The Governour,' written fifty years before Shakespeare's play. It seemed that a favourite servant of the Prince had been arraigned at the King's Bench, and the Prince came in a rage and demanded that he should be 'ungyued and sette at liberty.' But the Judge, Lord Chief Justice Gascoigne,

> sittyng styll without mouynge, declarynge the maiestie of the Kynges place of jugement hadde to the prince these words folowyng: Sir remembre your selfe; I kepe here the place of the King your soueraigne lorde and father. . . . And now for your contempt and disobedience go you to the prisone of the Kynges benche whereunto I committe you.[4]

In the old play *The Famous Victories of Henry V*, played as early as 1588, the Judge says, 'I commit you to the Fleete.' In the first English 'Life of Henry V' (1513) the above incident is not mentioned, but the author relates stories of robberies something like Shakespeare

---

[1] *a*. 1538. Starkey, *Life and Letters* (E.E.T.S.), 117.
[2] 1594. *A Knack how to know a Knave.*
[3] 1657. *Londinopolis*, p 362.
[4] 1531. *The Governour*, B. II. c. vi.

gives, but adds that the robbed persons were afterwards compensated.

Thomas Fuller gives a story characteristic of Sir Thomas More:

> When Sir Thomas More was Lord Chancellor of England and Sir John his father one of the judges of the Kings Bench, he would in Westminster Hall beg his blessing of him on his knees [1]

Wycherley in a play gives us a type of barrister happily passed away:

> Come Mr. Blunder, pray bawl soundly for me at the King's Bench, bluster, sputter, question, cavil; but be sure your argument be intricate enough to confound the Court; and then you do my business.[2]

Here is an instance where the Court was used for a criminal trial (1628):

> Felton (the murderer of the Duke of Buckingham) was arraigned and found guilty at the Kings-Bench Bar and hanged at Tyburn [3]

V

The High Court of Chancery is (to quote a late 17th century writer)

> placed next the Kings Bench as mitigating the Rigor thereof; this Court is the womb of all our fundamental Laws: it is called Chancery as some imagine because the Judge sat anciently *inter Cancellos* or within Lattices—this Court proceeds to grant Writs according to equity of Conscience.[4]

William Lambarde, however, in his 'Archeion,' goes a little further:

> He (the Chancellor) is said to cancel, deface or make void a Record ... by drawing certain crosse lines Lattice-wise with his Pen over it; whereby it is so enclosed or shut up that from thence forth no exemplifications thereof may be given abroad.[5]

---

[1] 1642. *The Holy State*, vi.
[2] c. 1667. *Plain Dealer*, III. i.
[3] Baker's *Chron.*, 'Chas. I,' 494.
[4] 1681. R. Burton, *Historic Remarques*, pt. i. p. 11.
[5] 1635. p 46.

COURT OF CHANCERY

The term Court of Conscience had long been in use when the above was written, and Cavendish in his 'Life of Wolsey' says it was in common use in his time

> because it hath jurisdiction to command the high ministers of the common-law to share execution and judgment, where conscience hath most effect.[1]

Francis Quarles thinks that an ideal Court of Conscience belonged to a 'golden age' long past:

> that golden age is gone
> There was no client then to wait
> The leisure of his long-tail'd advocate,
> The talion law was in request,
> And Chanc'ry courts were kept in every breast.[2]

In this Court Cromwell assumed the title of Lord Protector,

> being install'd with much formality and ceremony . . . in presence of the Judges, the Lord Mayor etc and the Chief Officers of the Army (1653)[3]

The 'State Papers of Charles I' afford an instance of a successful petitioner which might serve to stop the mouth of the trivial scorner who pretends to find an analogy between Chance and Chancery. Sir William Russell petitioned the Court, who had already decreed that his father-in-law should pay over £500, part of his wife's portion. The defendant, Sir Thomas Reade, although a man of large estate, disobeyed the order and had been in the Fleet for two years. For his contempt the Court had imposed fines of £1000. A subsequent entry in the same year (1631) records a 'Grant to Sir Wm Russell of 2 fines of £500 imposed that out of it he might receive satisfaction of £500 with costs.'[4]

---

[1] a 1557.
[2] 1634. *Emblems*, B. I.
[3] Baker's *Chron.* (1665), p. 673.
[4] *Cal. State Papers Chas. I. (Domestic)*, pp. 497 and 524.

A LITERARY TOPOGRAPHY OF OLD LONDON

VI

Originally the word Exchequer meant a chess-board, from the old French 'Eschequier.' To play the *escheker* was to play at chess. So Caxton in his 'Game and Playe of the Chesse,' 1474:

> Ther ben as many points in the eschequer voyde as fulle.

As to the Court so called, 'the name originally referred to the Abacus or table covered with a cloth divided into squares on which the accounts of the revenue were kept by means of counters.' 'Tallies' were also in use for this purpose. These were sticks split in half, the two halves being put together and notched at the junction to indicate payments.[1] James Howell in 'Londinopolis' is not strictly correct·

> The place was called Exchequer from a French word *une place quarrée* because the carpet which lay before the Judges is in the form of a chess-board and of two colours.[2]

But Camden has the facts correctly:

> Upon this Exchequer Board is laid a cloth reived with strikes distant one from another a foote.[3]

An early writer calls it:

> A place which was ordained only for the Kings revenue where two knights, two clerks and two learned men in the law are assigned to hear and determine wrongs done to the King and Crown in right of his fees [4]

Originally the Seasons, and then place of Audit, the word *Scaccarium*, or Exchequer, came presently to be used as the name of a Court which in time became famous. 'The pleading part on the one side and the paying part on the other side of Westminster Hall.' So Fuller writes in his 'Worthies,' and he goes on to allude to Queen Elizabeth,

who maintained her Exchequer that her Exchequer might maintain her.

---

[1] Hence the verb 'to tally' in modern use.   [2] 1657, p. 369.
[3] *Britannia* (1610), 1. 178 (tr. Holland).
[4] 1646. William Hughes, *Mirrour of Justices*, I. xiv. (trans. of a much earlier work).

COURT OF EXCHEQUER

'As sure as Exchequer pay' was a proverb which seems to indicate public confidence. Another proverb is of a different character. 'There is no redemption from Hell' referred to a debtors' prison under the Court named 'Hell.'

If we may judge from many references in the Drama and from other sources, the Court had not a high reputation for honest dealing.

In the early play of *Roister Doister*, by Nicholas Udall, who was Headmaster of Eton, we read:

> For sure I will put you up into the Eschequer.
> Why so? . . .
> For an usurer.[1]

And in a tract written about the same time:

> Oh that the kings grace knew of the extorcyon oppressyon and brybery that is used in his ij Courtys; that is to say of the Augmentacyon and of the Eschekei There hath bene moch speaking of the paynes of purgatory; but a man were as good in a maner to come into the paynes of hell as into eyther of those ij Courtys[2]

Falstaff in Shakespeare's *Henry IV* says

> Rob me the Exchequer the first thing thou do'st, and do it with unwash'd hands too.[3]

and a character in a play of Fletcher says much the same thing:

> but if you need
> Do things of danger . . .
> Rob the Exchequer and burn all the Rolls
> And these will make a shew.[4]

Robert Crowley gives a warning which would be an insult to a Judge in our day:

> If thou be a iudge in commune place
> In the Kinges bench or Exchequier
> Or other courte, let not thy face
> Be once turned to the Briber.[5]

---

[1] *a* 1553, V vi.
[2] *c* 1541. *The Complaynt of Roderyck Mors* (E E T S), p. 24.
[3] 1598, Part I   [4] 1639. *Wit without Money*, II. 1.
[5] 1550. *The Voyce of the last Trumpet*, l. 961 (E E.T S).

A LITERARY TOPOGRAPHY OF OLD LONDON

VII

The Court of Common Pleas, for the trial of civil actions at law, was in early times called 'Common-Place,' the word seemingly taken from 'Communia placita.' Lydgate uses it in the 15th century in his 'London Lyckpenny':

> Unto the common place I yode
> Where sat one with a sylken hoode.

It is used in 1546 in an Act, 37 Henry VIII, c. 19:

> The Chief Justices of the Common place.

Crowley's use of 'commune place' in 1550 has already been quoted.[1]

The Court is satirised by a poet of Charles the First's time:

> Then one grave Serieant of the Common Pleas
> Might well dispatch the motions at his ease
> And in his own hands though he had the Law
> Yet hardly had a Clyent worth a straw.[2]

Another reference may be cited from one of Wycherley's post-Restoration plays. He treats the subject in a vein of ridicule, as was not unusual when the Law or legal procedure was the topic

> Go then, go to your court of Common Pleas, and say one thing over and over again, you do it so naturally, you'll never be suspected for protracting time.[3]

William Lambarde in his 'Dictionarium' speaks of 'the place of Comon-Pleas within the Cytie called commonly the Guildhall'[4]

---

[1] P. 151, under 'Exchequer.'
[2] 1634 *Pasquil's Palinodia*, B. 3
[3] c. 1667. *Plain Dealer*, III. 1.
[4] a. 1601 (1730, p. 171).

COURT OF ARCHES

VIII

The chief Ecclesiastical Court of Appeal bore this name from its place of meeting, viz the Church of St. Mary-le-bow, i.e. St. Mary of the Arches. The Arches formed the Crypt of the Norman Church destroyed in the Great Fire. Parts of the Crypt, however, were spared, and may still be seen.

Cases of heresy were tried here as early as Henry V, if not earlier. Sir John Oldcastle is a case in point. The following extract is from the anonymous play bearing his name for title:

> He doth beside maintain a strange religion
> And will not be compelled to come to masse.
>
> (*Bishop of Rochester*)
> We do beseech you therefore gracious prince
> Without offence unto your maiesty,
> We may be bold to use authoritie
> To summon him unto the Arches
> Where such offences haue their punishment.[1]

Fulke Greville, in his 'Life of Sir Philip Sidney,' touches on the use of this Court in the Reign of Queen Elizabeth.

> For her clergy with their Ecclesiasticall or Civill jurisdictions, she fashioned the Arches, and Westminster Hall to take such care one to bound another that they in limiting themselves, enlarged her Royalties, as the chief and equall foundations of both their greatnesses[2]

In the 'State Papers' (Charles I, 1643) the case of a vicar unable to obtain his tithe is mentioned.

> Then the Court of Arches should give relief, and if not obeyed, the Common Law will and must assist them[3]

To revert to an earlier century, we find mention of the Court in a letter of John Paston in 1478:

> And as for Mastyr Pykenham he is now Juge of the Archys and also he hathe an other offyce which is callyd *Auditor Causarum*[4]

---

[1] 1600, I. 11. [2] a 1628 (pub. 1652).
[3] *Cal. State Papers Charles I (Domestic).*
[4] *Paston Letters*, No. 812.

A LITERARY TOPOGRAPHY OF OLD LONDON

IX

The building in Chancery Lane adjoining Serjeants' Inn and known as 'The Rolls,' and, subsequently, the Public Record Office,[1] was—to quote John Stow:

> Some time the house of the converted Jewes, founded by King Henry the third, in place of a Jewes house to him forfeited in the yeare 1233 . . .[2] who builded there for them a faire Church now used and called the Chappell for the Custodie of Rolles and Records of Chauncerie . . In the yeare 1377 this house was annexed by patent to William Burstall, Clearke, Custos Rotulorum or keeper of the Rolles of Chauncerie by Edwarde the third in 51 of his raigne and this first Maister of the Rolles was sworne in Westminster Hall at the Table of marble stone.[3]

In the early part of the 15th century John Lydgate writes

> Unto the Rolls I gat from thence
> Before the clarkes of the Chauncereye

But he found that a man with an empty pocket fared badly:

> Lacking money I could not be sped.[4]

It will be seen that fees were in Lydgate's time, as they have ever since been, charged for searching or making extracts from the public documents, whether kept at 'The Rolls' or the Tower or other places. The title-page of a book by Thomas Powell in 1622 runs

> Directions for search of Records remaining in the Chancerie, Tower, Exchequer, with the Limnes thereof . . . with the accustomed Fees of Search and diverse necessarie observations.

---

[1] The Record Office is not a Court of Justice, although the Master of the Rolls is *ex-officio* a Judge of Appeal. But as the National Repository of Public Records and State Papers reference to it is not entirely out of place in a paper treating of the Parliament Houses and other Courts of Law.

[2] This 'Domus Conversorum' is mentioned in the *Patent Rolls*, Jan 28, 1344 'Grant for Life to Janettus de Ispania, a convert, of such sustenance from the *Domus Conversorum* as the other Converts of that house have.'—*Calendar Edw. III*, p. 190.

[3] *Survey* (1603), pp. 395-6.

[4] *London Lyckpenny*, or 'Lackpenny,' c. 1430.

THE RECORD OFFICE

At a time when 'The Rolls' buildings in Chancery Lane were limited in space, many of the Public Records were kept in the Chapel of St. John in the Tower of London, and many historians and antiquaries went there for material

William Prynne, who gained an unpleasant reputation at an earlier period of his life, was Chief Keeper of the Records at the Tower, and Anthony à Wood in his Diary (June 22, 1667) writes:

> After that he (i e. Prynne) conducted A W into the White Tower, where he was strangely surprized to see such vast numbers of Charters and Rolls. . . . He found Mr. Dugdale in the office where he was to sit, who was running over a course of Rolls in order to drawing up . . Monasticon Anglicanum.

Elias Ashmole also writes in his Diary[1] that he went to 'the Record Office in the Tower' to collect materials for his 'Work of the Garter.'

William Lambarde was Keeper of the Records in the Rolls Chapel in 1597 and of those in the Tower in 1601, the year of his death. In his 'Archeion' he speaks of the Rolls as having been 'of long time, as it were, the Colledge of the Chancerie-men.'

Thomas Cromwell was Master before his disgrace. Michael Drayton makes him tell his story:

> For first from knighthood rising in degree,
> The office of the Jewel House my lot
> After the Rowles he frankly gave to mee
> From whence a prime Counseller I got.[2]

It was a strange place to choose for a public execution, yet we read in Walter Yonge's Diary

> The 3rd of May 1606, Garnet the provincial seminary . . . was executed at the west end of the Rolls [3]

[1] 1658 May 7
[2] *The Legend of Great Cromwell* (1609), p 22
[3] Henry Garnett was a Jesuit accused of complicity in the Gunpowder Plot

A LITERARY TOPOGRAPHY OF OLD LONDON

X

James Howell in 'Londinopolis' touches on the importance of the Court of Admiralty:

- Great Britain being an Island which makes the Sea and Woodden Castles to be her Chiefest Conservators, the Court of Admiralty may be said to be more pertinent and necessary to her, then to divers other States.[1]

In early times it was presided over by the Lord High Admiral[2] Later we find the Judge alluded to, and Pepys speaks of Sir Thomas Exeter who was both Judge of the Admiralty Court and Dean of the Arches, and he relates how he went

To St Margaret's Hill Southwark where the Judge of the Admiralty come . . . The charge given by Dr Exton methought was somewhat dull . . . Justice had two wings one of which spread itself over the land and the other over the water which was this Admiralty Court[3]

According to Blackstone the Court was one not only of civil jurisdiction but also of criminal, and we read in Harrison's ' Description of Britain ':

Pirates and robbers by sea are condemned in the Court of the Admiralty and hanged on the shore at low-water mark, where they are left till three tides have overwashed them.[4]

XI

As a criminal court, Newgate, familiarly known as the 'Old Bailey,' was the best known. Thomas Kyd, the poet, writing of the murder of John Brewen, says:

Then shee and Parker were both araigned and condemned . . . at the Sessions hall nere Newgate; and the woman had judgement to be burned in Smythfield and the man to be hanged in the same place before her eyes.[5]

---

[1] 1657, p 373
[2] W. Lambarde in his *Archeion* says, 'I think that the decision of Marine Causes was not put out of the King's House and committed over to the charge of the Admirall untill the time of King Edward the Third'
[3] *Diary*, March 17, 1662-3 The Court was a part of the disused Church of St Margaret. See also *Oxford Dictionary*
[4] 1577, B. III. c. vi.   [5] 1592 *Works* (1901), p 293.

HICKS' HALL

A Match in Newgate is the title of a 17th century play.

> To-morrow is the Sessions at the Old-Bailey. I'll make him shrink with fear ere I have done.[1]

William Lilly, the astrologer (so called), has the following allusion:

> The young man indicted him for a cheat at the Old-Baily. . . . Some of the Bench enquired what Hart did; he sat like an Alderman in his gown, quoth the fellow; at which the Court fell into great laughter most of the Court being Aldermen.[2]

Hicks' Hall in Clerkenwell afterwards became known as the Sessions House.

In the tenth year of James I, writes Sir Richard Baker in his ' Chronicle ':

> Sir Baptist Hicks, who was afterwards Viscount Campden, built a faire Sessions House of brick and stone in St. John Street which by the Justices was called after his name Hicks' Hall [3]

James Howell adds an encomium:

> What a large, noble soul had Sir Baptist Hicks, Lord Viscount Campden, what a number of worthy things did he in his life! [4]

William Lilly in his Autobiography relates an unpleasant experience.

> In 1655 I was indicted at Hicks' Hall by a half-witted young woman . . . for that I had given Judgment upon stollen Goods and received 2s. 6d.[5]

Samuel Butler in ' Hudibras ' tells of ' A Lawyer ':

> An old dull sot; wh' had told the Clock,
> For many years at Bridewell-Dock
> At Westminster and Hickes-Hall.

But perhaps the most important criminal trial was

---

[1] 1680. Betterton, founded on Marston's *Dutch Courtezan* (1605).
[2] c. 1660. *Autobiography* (1715, p 25). See also *Id.*, p 39.
[3] 1643, p. 151.
[4] *Londinopolis*, p 406.
[5] 1715, p. 73.

that of the Regicides, which took place a few months after the Restoration :

> The Proceedings at Hicks'-Hall Tuesday the 9th of October 1660 in order to the Trial of the Pretended Judges of his Late Sacred Majesty.[1]

Mention is made of a small Court, viz. that of the Marshall, by W. Lambarde in his ' Archeion ' :

> The Court of the Constable or Marshall of England determineth Contracts touching Deeds of Armes out of the Realme and handleth things concerning Warre within the Realme, as Combats, Blazon, Armorie, etc.[2]

The following is an earlier reference ·

> The Court of Marshalsea is an ancient Court and made for the well-government of the King's house The Coroner of the Marshalsea shall sit with the Coroner of the County upon the death of a man [3]

A contemporary writer makes a complaint

> I can neyther thynck, speake, nor write, the slendernesse and unreasonable chargys of that court.[4]

The writer, Henry Brinkelow, who had been a Franciscan friar, gave up the Order and took to trade and the writing of Satires on the abuses of the time. Happily such treatment as prisoners had to endure four centuries ago has long been abolished.

---

[1] *Indictment of the Regicides.*
[2] 1635, p. 43.
[3] 1646. W Hughes, *Mirrour of Justices*, trans of a much earlier work
[4] c. 1541 Henry Brinkelow, *Complaynt of Roderick Mors* (E E.T S), p. 26.

Index of Authors Quoted

In the case of anonymous works the Titles are indexed.

ALLEYN, Edward, 88
Archæologia, 47
Ashmole, Elias, 155
Aubrey, John, 60
Aulicus Coquinariæ, 95, 97

BACON, Sir Francis, 31, 36, 142, 145
Bacon, Sir Nicholas, 126
Baker, Sir Richard, 10, 17, 23, 34, 57, 68, 96, 105, 144, 145, 148, 149
Bale, John, 58
Barclay, Alexander, 140
Barry, Lodowick, 145
Bassompierre, Marshall de, 19, 113
Behn, Mrs Aphra, 104
Benlowes, Edward, 43
Betterton, Thomas, 157
Birch, T, 102
'The Black Conclave of Conspirators at Derby House,' 125
Blackstone, Sir William, 156
Boorde, Andrew, x
Broadside, 3
Browne, E, 22
'Brut' (Chronicle), ix
Burnet, Bishop, 100, 102, 108
Burton, R, 148
Butler, Samuel, 57, 111, 157

CALENDAR, Charter Rolls, 76, 124
Calendar, Close Rolls, 7, 66, 133
Calendar, Letters and Papers Henry VII, 60, 61, 77
Calendar, Letters and Papers Henry VIII, 16, 24, 25, 121
Calendar, Patent Rolls, 5, 6, 66, 76, 121, 154
Calendar, State Papers, Domestic, 13, 80, 96, 149, 153
Calendar, Venetian State Papers, 69
Camden, Sir William, ix, 7, 100, 150

Campeggio, Cardinal, 69
Capgrave, John, 36
Carew Papers, 86
Carpenter, Richard, 27
Cary, Robert, 87
Cavendish, George, 24, 25, 51, 70, 149
Caxton, William, 150
Cecil, Sir Robert, 86, 94, 105
Chamberlain, John, 85, 90
Charles I, King, 20
'Cheque Book, The Old,' 23
Chester, Robert, ix
'Chronicles of London' (Cotton MSS), 15
'Chronicle of London,' 31, 54
Clarendon, Earl of, 14, 20, 21, 86, 93, 107
Clarendon State Papers, 100
Clarke Papers, 107, 143
Cowley, Abraham, 13, 21, 22
Cox, Thomas, 92
Cromwell, Oliver, 18
Cromwell, Thomas, 132
Crowley, Robert, 151
'Crown Garland of Golden Roses,' 33

DANIEL, Samuel, 5
Davenant, Sir William, 112
Davies, Sir John, 146
'Declaration of Treason of the Earl of Essex,' 85, 105
Dekker, Thos, 8, 9, 49
'The Divell of Derby House' (Tract), 125
Domesday Book, 102
Donne, John, 105
Dorset, Earl of. *See* Sackville, Thomas
Drayton, Michael, 8, 76, 155
Drue, Thomas, 128
Dugdale, Sir William, 48, 97
Dunbar, William, x

INDEX OF AUTHORS QUOTED

'Edward VI, Journal of,' 87
Egerton Papers, 58, 79
Elizabeth, Queen, 63
Elyot, Sir Thomas, 89, 147
Evelyn, John, 7, 21, 22, 37, 44, 82, 93, 98, 109, 127
'Execution of Justice on England,' 54

Fabyan, Robert, 17, 26, 68, 134
Fairfax, Bryan, 81, 82, 108
Ferrers, George, 34
Feuillerat, 19
Finett, Sir John, 81
Fisher's Folly, Lady Monk's Entertainment (Broadside), 110
Fitz-Stephen, William, 4
Ford, John, 36
'Four Fugitives' Meeting' (Tract), 120
Fuller, Thomas, 13, 25, 56, 96, 148

Gaimar, Geoffrey, 4
Gauden, Dr. John, xi
Gerard, John, 132
Gough, W., 77
Gregory, William, 67-8
Greville, Sir Fulke, 153

Hakewill, W., 142
Hamilton, Count Anthony, 13
Harington, Sir John, xi, 144
Harleian MSS, 51, 52
Harrison, William, 19, 36, 71, 137
Hatfield Papers (Calendar), 94
'Hatton Letters,' 11
Hayward, Sir John, 59, 63, 70, 90, 134
Henry VII, King, Will of, 27
Henslowe, Philip, 19
Hentzner, Paul, 34, 35, 142
Herbert of Cherbury, Lord, 46, 50
Herbert, Sir Thomas, vi, 11, 100
Herrick, Robert, x
Heylin, Dr Peter, 59, 134
Heywood, Thomas, 76
Holinshed, Raphael, 32
Howell, James, 32, 64, 138, 147, 157
Hughes, William, 150
Hutchinson, Colonel, 107

Ingulfus, 4

James I, King, 142
James II, King, 92
'Jane, Queen, Chronicle of,' 90
Johnson, Richard, 110
Jonson, Ben, 10, 80, 146

Kilburne, Richard, 33
King, Bishop Henry, 125-6
'A Knack to know a Knave,' 147
Kyd, Thomas, 156

Lambarde, William, 34, 144, 148, 152
'Lambeth's Faire's ended' (Tract), 46
Laud, William, Archbishop, 44, 45, 46, 80, 138, 142
Leland, John, 17, 88
Lilly, William, 157
'Litany, The Duke of Buckingham's,' 82
Lloyd, David, 88
'London, Chronicle of,' 70, 75, 78
'Lords, House of, Journal,' 94, 143, 144
'Ludlow, Edward, Memoirs,' 14, 107, 140, 143
Lupton, Thomas, xi
Lydgate, John, 152, 154
Lyly, John, x

Mabinogion, x
Machyn, Henry, 18, 19, 54, 93
Manningham, John, 95
Marvell, Andrew, 11, 108, 126
'Masques of the Inner Temple,' 59
May, Thomas, 30
Mercurius Politicus, 82
'Mirror for Magistrates,' 55
More, Sir Thomas, 118
Mors, Roderigo, 141, 151
'Motives for founding an University in London,' 55

Nalson, J., 20
Nash, Thomas, 140
Newcastle, Margaret, Duchess of, 83
Nicholas' 'Chronicle,' 26
Norden, John, xi, 71, 79, 139
North, Sir John, 55

Oldcastle, Sir John, anon. play, 153
Osborne, Dorothy, 100
Osborne, Francis, 97

INDEX OF AUTHORS QUOTED

Parker, Archbishop, 90
Parker, Martin, 11
Parliament, Acts of, 51
'Parliaments, Summary of,' 119
'Pasquil's Palinodia,' 152
Paston, John, 153
'Paston Letters,' 31
Pegge, Samuel, 4
'Pell Records,' 6
Pennant, Thomas, 42, 69
Pepys, Samuel, 14, 35, 47, 78, 100, 104, 127, 156
Peyton, Sir Edward, 13
Pole, Cardinal, 147
'Political Poems,' 26
'Preservation of four Worthy and Honourable Peeres,' etc. (Tract), 86
'Privy Council, Acts of,' 9, 104
Procter, J., 16, 58
Prynne, William, 141

Quarles, Francis, 148

Raleigh, Sir Walter, 90
'Raleigh, Sir Walter, Proceedings against,' 6
'Raleigh, Sir Walter, Arraignment of,' 91
'Regicides, The Indictment of,' 158
'Remembrancia,' 105
Rich, Barnabee, 140
'Richard III, True Tragedy of,' 54, 77
Roper, W., 50
Roy, W., 49
Royston, R., 139
Rugge, Thomas, 15, 82, 106, 109, 111, 114, 123
'Rump Songs,' 64, 81, 91
Rymer's 'Fœdera,' 121

Sackville, Thomas, 83
Scoble Collection, 143
Selden, John, 59
Shakespeare, William, 25, 27, 57, 62, 76, 118, 129, 146, 151

Shirley, James, 101
Sidney, Sir Henry, 90
'Sidney Papers,' 61
Sidney, Sir Philip, 84
Smyth, Sir Thomas, 139, 144
'Somers' Tracts,' 77
Spenser, Edmund, 85
Starkey, Thomas, Letters, 122, 147
Stow, John, 4, 6, 7, 8, 28, 29, 53, 58, 63, 66, 69, 76, 84, 92, 94, 95, 98, 99, 101, 110, 117, 122, 124, 127, 130, 137, 138, 141, 154
Suckling, Sir John, 97

Taylor, John, 64
Townsend, A., 10
Tusser, Thomas, xi
Tyndale, W., 49

Udall, Nicholas, 151

Vergil, Polydore, 54
Vicars, John, 44, 59

Waller, Edmund, 17, 21
Walsingham, Sir Francis, 84, 120
Walton, Isaak, 43, 105
Warkworth, John, 53
Webster, John, 78
Weldon, Sir A., 145
'Westminster Projects' (Tract), 125
Whitelock, James, 85
Whyte, Rowland, 78
Wilson, Arthur, 103
Wolsey, Cardinal, 69
Wood, Anthony à, 155
Wotton, Sir Henry, 106, 107
Wriothesley's 'Chronicle,' 82
Wycherley, William, 148, 152

Yonge, Walter, 23, 133, 155

'Zurich Letters,' 56

General Index

ABERGAVENNY House, 126
Admiralty, Court of, 156
Angus, Earl of, 77-8
Anne, Queen, 37
Arches, Court of, 153
Arundel House, 87-9
Arundel, Thomas, Bishop of Ely, 61-2
Ashmole, Elias, 155

BANGOR House, 67
Banqueting Hall of Whitehall, 10
Bath, Order of, 7
Bath Place, 69-70
Baynard Castle, 75-9
Beaudesert See Paget
Beaufort House, 92
Beaufort family, 93
Beck, Anthony de, 71
Bedford House, 93-4
Bell Tower at Westminster, 7
Berkeley House, 109
Berkeley House, Clerkenwell, 109-10
Berkeley Inn, Thames Street, 109
Bermondsey Abbey, 132
Bishops' Palaces, 41-71
'Blanche Chaumbre,' 7
Bloomsbury House, 133
Bohemia, Queen of, 106
Boleyn, Anne, 50
Boniface of Savoy, Archbishop, 42
Booth, Laurence, Archbishop, 48
Bowling Green, the, Whitehall, 15
Brandon, Charles, Duke of Suffolk, 52
Bridewell Palace, 24-5
Brooke House, 101-2
Buckingham, Duke of. See Villiers
Buckingham House, 101
Bull, the Pope's, against Queen Elizabeth, 54, 55
Burgh, Hubert de, 48
Burleigh House, 95-6
Burley, Sir Simon, his house, 124
Bury, Richard de, 71
Bygod House, 124

CAMPDEN House, 114
Campden, Viscount. See Sir Baptist Hicks
Campeggio, Cardinal, 69-70
Capgrave, John, 36
Capuchin Friars in London, 20
Carlisle, Bishop of, 93
Carlisle House, 61
Cavendish, William, Duke of Newcastle, 83
Cecil House, 94
Cecil, Sir Robert, Earl of Salisbury, 94-5
Cecil, Thomas, Earl of Exeter, 95
Cecil, Sir William, Baron of Burleigh, 95
Chancery, Court of, 148-9
Chapel of 'The Rolls,' 155
Charles I, execution of, 11
Charles I, King, trial of, 7
Chaucer, Geoffrey, 8
Chelsea, Palace at, 32
Chester and Coventry, the Bishop's Inn, 70
Chicheley, Henry, Archbishop, 42
Chichester Place, 66
Clarence, Duke of, 118, 122
Clarendon, Earl of, 92, 93
Clarendon House, St. James's, 93, 108, 109
Cockpit, the, Whitehall, 14
Cold Harbour, 121
Committee of Safety, 107
Common Pleas, Court of, 151, 152
Commons, the House of, 131
Constable, Court of the, 158
Contempt of Court, 149
Converted Jews, House of, 154
Cope, Sir William, 112
Copt Hall, 123
Cotton House, 99, 100
Cotton, Sir John, 100
Cotton, Sir Robert, 100
Courtenay, Edward, Earl of Devonshire, 111
Courtenay, Hugh, Earl of Devon, his house, 83

163

GENERAL INDEX

Courts of Justice, 144-58
Cox, Richard, Bishop of Ely, 63
Cromwell, Oliver, Lord Protector, 149
Cromwell, Oliver, funeral of, 21
Cromwell's daughter, marriage of, 13
Cromwell, Thomas, 131-2
Cromwell, Thomas (Master of the Rolls), 155
Crosby, Sir John, 117-19

DANVERS (or Davers), Charles, 105
David's, St, the Bishop's Place, 66
Deanery of St. Paul's, 57
Denbigh, Earl of, Speaker, 144
Denmark House, 23
Derby House, 125-6
Devereux, Robert, Earl of Essex, 79, 85-6
Devonshire House, Bishopsgate, 110
Devonshire House, Piccadilly, 109
Digby, Sir Kenelm, 59
Domus Conversorum, 154
Dorset House, 83
Drury, Elizabeth, 105
Drury House, 104, 105, 106
Drury, Sir Robert, 104, 105
Dudley, Edmund (Speaker of the House of Commons), 131
Dugdale, Sir William, 155
Durham College, 71
Durham House, 89, 90
Durham Palace 71,

EDWARD, the Black Prince, 62
Edward, the Black Prince, his house, 123
Edward IV, 53, 76
Edward V, 53, 54
Edward VI, 37, 52, 87, 89, 90
Egerton, Lord Chancellor, 79
Elizabeth, Queen, 9, 19, 34, 35, 37, 63, 85, 90, 130, 134
Ely House, 61-5
Eltham Palace, 32
Empson, Sir Richard, 131
'The Erber' (or Herbore), 122
Essex House, 80, 85, 86
Eton College, 16
Exchange, the new, 91
Exchequer, Court of, 150, 151
Exeter Change, 96
Exeter House, 84
Exeter House, Strand, 95
Exeter Palace, 68-9

FAIRFAX, Lord, 81
Fawkes, Guy, 142
Featly, Dr Daniel, 45
Felton, John, 55
Finch, Heneage, 37
Finland, Duke of, 59
Fisher, Bishop of Rochester, 61
Fisher's Folly, 110, 111
FitzAlan, Richard, Earl of Arundel, 89
Fitzwalter, Lord Robert, 76
Fulham Palace, 55-8
Furnival, Sir William, his house, 102

GARNETT, Henry, execution of, 155
Garter House, Barbican, 127
Gate-House, the, Westminster, 5
George the Traveller, 110
Gerard, John, herbalist, 104
Glanville, Bishop of Rochester, 42
Gondomar Court, 64
Goring House, 100
Great Houses of the Nobles and Statesmen, 75-114
Greenwich Palace, 9, 33-5
Gresham House, 120
Gresham, Sir Thomas, 119-20
Greville, Sir Fulke, 101-2
Grey, Lady Jane, 78, 90
Guise, Mary of, 54
Gunpowder Plot, 142, 155
Guy, Earl of Warwick, 103

HAMPTON Court, 30
Hardiknut, 42
Hatton House, 101
Heath, Archbishop, 52
Henrietta Maria, Queen, 19, 21
Henry VI, King, 6, 53, 76
Henry VII, King, 77
Henry VIII, King, 33, 50, 51, 70, 80
Henry VIII, marriage of, 68
Herbert, William, Viscount Powis, 102
Hereford, the Bishop's place, 66
Hicks, Sir Baptist, 114, 157
Hicks' Hall, 157-8
Holbein Gate, 14
Holland House, 112, 113
Holland, John, Earl of Huntingdon, 121
Holland, Philemon, 110
Hollar, Wenceslaus, 9, 91, 94
Howard House (Charter House), 126

GENERAL INDEX

Howard, Philip, 87
Humphrey, Duke of Gloucester, 76
Hyde, Anne, 92

JAMES I, King, 10, 80, 95, 97, 142
James II, King, 17, 92
James's Fair, St., 15
James-the-less, St., Sisterhood of, 15
James's Palace, St., 15-18
Jones, Inigo, 10
Juxon, Bishop, 56, 57

KATHERINE of Arragon, Queen, 70
Kensington Palace, 37
King's Bench, Court of, 146-8
King's Head Tavern, 104
Knollys, Sir William, Earl of Banbury and Viscount Wallingford, 106

LACY, Henry, Earl of Lincoln, 83
Lambeth Palace, 41-7
Langton, Walter, Bishop, 70
Laud, William, Archbishop, 43, 44, 57
Leicester House, 84
Leicester, Robert Dudley, Earl of, 84, 85, 130
Leighton, Alexander, 46-7
Leper Hospital, St James's, 15
Library at Durham College, 71
Library at St. James's, 18
Library at Lambeth, 45, 46
Library, the Portcus, 57
Library, Sir Robert Cotton's, 100
Lichfield, Bishop of, 70
Lincoln Place, 65
Lincoln, Earl of, his house, 83
Lindsey House, 103
Llandaff, the Bishop's Place, 67
Lollards' Tower, 42
London House, 53-5
Lord Mayor's Show, 19
Lords, House of, 143, 144

MANCHESTER, Lord, 104
Maps of London, xi
Margaret, Queen of James IV of Scotland, 77
Marie de Medici, 17
Marshalsea, the Court of, 158
Mary, Queen, 16, 37, 52, 134
Mayfair, 15
Merchant Taylors' School, 130
Monk, General, 107, 110

Montagu, Edward, Earl of Manchester, 104
Montague House, Bloomsbury, 133
Montague House, Southwark, 132
Monteagle House, 133
More, Sir Thomas, 118
Mounthaunt family, 66

NEVILLE, Ralph, Bishop of Chichester, 66
Neville, Richard, Earl of Warwick, 103
Newcastle House, 103
Newcastle House, Clerkenwell, 127
Newgate as a Criminal Court, 156
Northampton House (afterwards Suffolk), 97
Northumberland, Duke of, 90
Northumberland House, Aldersgate Street, 98
Northumberland House (formerly Suffolk), 97, 98
Nottingham House, 37
Nursery, a Royal, 37

OLD BAILEY, 156
Old Jewry, Palace in, 29
Orange, Prince of, 10
Oxford, Earl of, his house in Candlewick Street, 130

PAGET House, 84
Paget, William, Baron of Beaudesert, 84
Painted Chamber, the, 140
Parker, Archbishop, 47
Parliament Houses, 137-44
Parr, Queen Katherine, 87
Philip, ' King,' 134
Pindar, Sir Paul, his house, 120
Pirates, the punishment of, 156
' Placentia.' *See* Greenwich Palace
Pole, Margaret (Countess of Salisbury), 122-3
Pollexfen House, 129
Popham, Lord Chief Justice, 142
Printing House, the King's, 98-9
Prynne, William, 44, 155
Public Record Office, 154-5
Pulteney, Sir John, 89, 121

RALEIGH, Sir Walter, 90, 91
Reade, Sir Thomas, 149
Records in the Tower, 155
Regicides, trial of the, 158
Rich, Robert, Earl of Warwick, 104
Richard II, 138

GENERAL INDEX

Richard III, 76, 118
Richmond, Palace of, 31
Rivers, Margaret de, Countess of Devon, 112
Rochester House, 42, 60, 61
'Rolls, The,' 132, 154
Rose Manor, 129
Russell, Sir William, 149
Rutland House, 112

SACKVILLE House, 83
Salisbury, Earl of. *See* Cecil, Sir Robert
Salisbury Palace, 67–8
Savoy, the, 25, 28
Scrope House, 124
Scrope Inn, Holborn, 124
Seymour Place, 87
Sheldon, William, 47
Shelley, Sir William, 51
Shene Palace, 31
Shrewsbury House, 121
Sidney, Sir Henry, 90
Sidney, Sir Philip, 90
Somerset, Duke of, Protector, 18
Somerset, Edward, Earl of Worcester, 92
Somerset House, 18–24
'Somerset Inn' (Thames St.), 79
Southampton, Earl of, 127. *See* Wriothesley
Southampton House, 82, 104
Stapleton, Walter, Bishop of Exeter, 68–9
Star Chamber, 144, 146
Sudeley, Thomas Seymour, Baron of, 87
Suffolk House, Barbican, 128
Suffolk House, Minories, 128
Suffolk House (formerly Northampton), 97
Suffolk Place, Southwark, 134
Sussex, Earl of, house in Bermondsey, 132

TEMPLE, the old, 65–6
Theobalds Palace, 32
The Tennis Court, Whitehall, 14

The Tilt Yard, Whitehall, 14
Tiptoft, John, Earl of Worcester, 91
Totenhall, Manor House, 102
Tower of London as a Royal Residence, 36, 37

UNIVERSITY for London, 55

VERE, DE, family, 130–1
Verulam, Viscount. *See* Bacon
Villiers, George, Duke of Buckingham, 80
Visscher's Views, 79

WALLINGFORD House, 106, 107
Wallingford, Viscount, 106
Walter, Hubert, Archbishop, 42
Warwick House, Cloth-Fair, 112
Warwick House, Holbourne, 103
Warwick Inn, Newgate Street, 103, 111
Westminster Hall, 4, 137–40
Westminster Palace, 3–8, 137
Weston, Sir Richard, 105, 106
Whitehall Palace, 9–15
'White Hall' (in old Westminster Palace), 7
Whittington's Palace, 133
William the Conqueror, 4
William Rufus, 4
William III, 37
Wimbledon House, 96
Winchester House, 58–60
Windsor Castle, 30
Wolsey, Cardinal, 49, 50, 51, 69, 70
Worcester, the Bishop's Inn, 70
Worcester House, Strand, 92, 93
Worcester House, Thames Street, 91–2
Wriothesley, Henry, 83
Wriothesley, Sir John, 128
Wriothesley, Sir Thomas, 127

YORK House, 48–52
York House, Charing Cross, 79–82
York House in Southwark, 52

Milton Keynes UK
Ingram Content Group UK Ltd.
UKHW020711291124
3247UKWH00018B/135